PLAYING BY THE RULES

PLAYING BY THE RULES

JUSTIN ELZIE

QUEER MOJO
A Rebel Satori Imprint
Bar Harbor, Maine

REBEL SATORI PRESS
P.O. Box 363
Hulls Cove, ME 04644

This memoir depicts real events and is true and accurate to the best recollection and knowledge of the author.

Book design by Sven Davisson
Cover Photo: Randy Davey

ISBN-13: 978-1-60864-042-3

Printed in the U.S.A.

Some people spend an entire lifetime wondering if they made a difference in the world. But, the Marines don't have that problem.

—Ronald Reagan, President of the United States; 1985

Something has changed within me, something is not the same, I'm through with playing by the rules of someone else's game, Too late for second guessing, Too late to go back to sleep, It's time to trust my instincts, Close my eyes and leap

—Song: "Defying Gravity"

This book is dedicated to John Logan, who was the only Marine that was there with me through all the hard times and the good times. Without him I could not have made it through this ordeal.

FOREWORD

For those working in the struggle for full equality, it is so easy to become captive to statistics, data and timelines to prove our worthiness to be first class American citizens. Activists follow phone trees, email campaigns and briefing papers to make us better prepared for the epic civil rights struggle we are fighting on a daily basis. We can easily recite that over 13,000 of our courageous lesbian, gay, bisexual, and transgender soldiers have been dismissed from the military since President Clinton handed us "Don't Ask, Don't Tell." The community has had to listen to countless politicians explain while now is not the time, and offer pitiful excuses, for their own lack of courage to repeal this draconian policy. Often, in our eagerness for acceptance, we have forgiven unforgivable political conduct.

What is missing from this equation is our own humanity. The powerful stories of fear and oppression that have emerged from this long journey to be free are missing in action. Some because many of our possible storytellers have died in the dark period of AIDS, and are no longer around to remind us of our remarkable history, and some because they couldn't tell their stories. You are about to read of one Marine that wasn't asked, but told.

Young people often are shocked that lobotomies were a common practice in the 1950's. City police in every part of the country often raided political meetings of the gay and lesbian community in the 1960's. In reading the history of the HIV/AIDS epidemic they are stunned to discover that our government not only failed to fight this epidemic, but let it spread because it started in the gay community.

In many tribes in Africa, the role of the 'storyteller' is one of the most honored. The Sage that passes down to future generations the tales of bravery, courage, and our own unique "trail of tears," holds an esteemed place within the community. So many of our most articulate storytellers that could inspire this generation of activists were taken from us by the plague of HIV/AIDS. Those who emerged from the 1980's and 1990's still alive, even have a greater responsibility to share their journey to inspire the next generation.

As I read Justin Crockett Elzie's Playing by the Rules, I breathed a huge sigh of relief in knowing that one more powerful story has been effectively and creatively saved for our youth. The easy path for Justin would have been just to share his coming out process in the military. Many of us, abstractly, can recite the familiar tale of fear, decision making and the process of coming out. In the military, the feeling is even more intense with the inevitable hearings, shunning and discharge from your life's calling. The sense of hope and pride of having found truth within one's self is even a more difficult path.

However to start at that point is to leave so much out of our struggle for freedom. The struggle begins with our birth, that early awareness, those first man crushes (usually on television) and the erotic moments of our first exploration. Those are the stories that create the man who is able to reach deep inside himself, and insist on living as a free man with dignity and honor. The moments of fear in our childhood and the stark loneliness is engraved into so many of our stories. The horror of possible exposure and the deep intense desires that we feel in our loins.

Justin Crockett Elzie has written a remarkable book. His story should be read not only by our activists, but by every American. The beginning of his journey, on the plains of Wyoming, born to devoutly religious parents, to finding his identity in being a Marine is powerful. Every step of the way, Justin relives his pain with brutal honesty to ensure that we miss nothing of his struggle.

I am mesmerized by his childhood in the Wyoming prairies. The constant battle of being forced to stand up for himself against bullies and emotional terrorists is jolting. Justin had to be strong from Day One. In those windswept plains, it was just him attempting to come to terms with his homosexuality in the most hostile environment that you can imagine. Parents who were abusive to not only him but also his sister made difficult any search for truth. By the end of this book, each and every one reading it, their heart will ache with the pains of his journey. However, not one of you will view Justin as a victim. Because in the end, he is victorious and is living as a free man who has more honor and dignity than most other Marines.

This is a book for the ages, and I am in awe at Justin's courage in writing it and sharing it with us. The best way we can honor his journey, and his courage, is by sharing his story far and wide.

David Mixner

ACKNOWLEDGEMENTS

This book is a piece of my life, something that I knew that I had to finish in order to make a difference, and there are a few people that I need to thank. Without their help and support I could not have finished this book. I first want to thank my two editors, David Badash, who is a writer and the man behind the gay rights website, The New Civil Rights Movement, and John Shields, who is an Air Force veteran and writer. These two men took time out of their busy lives to painstakingly go through the manuscript, edit it, and give me constructive feedback on its content, grammar and style. I owe them both an immense debt of gratitude.

I next want to thank my publisher, Sven Davisson, with Rebel Satori Press, who has given me this opportunity to tell my story, and who took a chance on this book. He has made this whole process of publishing smooth and effortless. He has been amazing to work with.

I would be remiss if I didn't thank my heroes through this whole ordeal, my attorneys, Lanny Breuer, Christopher Sipes, Allan Moore, Lieutenant William Brown and the law firm of Covington & Burling. These men were there for me when nobody else was and they stuck by me. They were my counselors, my champions, who stood up to bigotry, and in the face of an enemy that was relentless, they were true warriors. I will forever be in their debt.

Along the way, close friends have been strongly supportive of this project and have taken time out in their lives to be a part of this journey. Nikos Kontomaris, Lisa Budwig and Darry Johnson, all read through the manuscript and gave me detailed, useful feedback and advice. This book would not have been possible without their moral support and encouragement in this project.

In reading this book you will find out that my true twin in my life is my sister Becky. She has been a sounding board, a counselor, and guide in my life journey. She kept me honest and on the path in my journey writing this book. I would not be the man I am today without her.

Also along the way I have had friends in my life that have given me useful advice and have been incredibly supportive of me in this process. Patrick Wallen, Rich Merritt, Perry Dean Young, Tanya Domi, Gene Barfield, Piero Savio, Jo Ann Santangelo, Jon Winkleman, Vincent Cianni, Jim Palmer, Bill Brooks, Jim Vivyan, David John Fleck, Daniel Handal, and Mario Braga. I have to also thank Kathy and Tad Hendrickson for giving me a quiet space to write and get my thoughts in order. This was essential to this project. I need to thank my roommate Kyle for his help this year. I would not have been able to complete this project without it.

I would also like to thank Mike Nichols for reading the manuscript and giving me constructive feedback on it. Mike has been a great teacher and I really appreciated his words of wisdom.

I would be in trouble if I didn't thank the Drag Queens of Friends Lounge that put up with so much living in a military town and supporting their Marines. Danny Leonard, aka "Brandy Alexander," "Secret," "Donna Saye," and "Scarlett Dailey." I found out that we all can learn something from a brave and ballsy Drag Queen.

I also need to thank those men who came into my life at crucial points and helped me become the man I am today: Jack Clayton, Kel Stiles, Len Regan, John Conte, Eduardo, Michael Degutis, Jim Heiser, Joe Granger, Glenn Hargett, Nikos Kontomaris, Steven Wainio, and John Logan.

And lastly I want to thank the other side. As we grow as spiritual beings we find out that those who have gone on before us are on the other side and are still in our lives daily, helping us and guiding us. So I above all need to thank my spirit guide and those on the other side. Without their encouragement and messages that I needed to finish this book to make a difference in people's lives, it would not have been done. Thank you.

CHAPTER 1
WALKING ACROSS THE DIVIDE

0530 hours 29 January 1993 Camp Lejeune, North Carolina

As I lay in bed I thought of the day ahead of me. Turning over on my side I looked at John sleeping next to me. My heart ached because I loved him so much and he looked so vulnerable and yet extremely angry with what I was about ready to do. I had an apprehension that only a recruit on his first night at boot camp would appreciate. Since being presented a couple of days ago with the opportunity of coming out and making the decision on Thursday, I had an instinctive internal drive, almost animal like, to come out in a public way, and nothing was going to stop me. I felt like I was on a train to destiny that I couldn't get off, even if I wanted to.

The thing is though, it was something that I felt I had to do no matter what the consequences. Some people may understand this, but the decision to come out was above all a deeply spiritual experience to the point I felt it was like a baptism in the making. I was finally going to stand up to the United States Marine Corps and let them know who the real Justin Elzie was and how screwed up the ban on gays in the military was. I wanted to make a positive difference and change the Marine Corps. But before that was to happen I had to get to work and make sure everything went as planned. I had a strategy and a plan and I had to make sure it went well.

I got out of bed, showered, put on my uniform and met John in the kitchen. He asked me if I was still going to come out today on national television, ABC World Evening News broadcast. When I said "yes," he threw the coffee cup that he was holding into the sink, breaking it. He looked like he was about ready to breakdown as he walked back to the bedroom not saying a word to me. I stood there in the kitchen distressed as I knew there was nothing that I could say to get him to come to terms with my decision. Being my boyfriend he was the most important person in my life and yet I couldn't get him to support me in this.

What I was going to do would affect him also. Being my room-mate, people in the Marine Corps would suspect him as being gay. In the military there is this idea that if someone hangs around or lives with someone who is gay, then they are gay as well. "Guilt by association" is what it is called, and that was what was about ready to happen to John.

What made this situation even more stressful for both of us was that John was gay. Being a fellow Marine who was also my boy-friend, we couldn't let anyone in the Marine Corps know, so that his life was not ruined. However, just by associating with me he would be affected and would be under suspicion. In effect I would be outing him as well, hence his distress over the situation, which was clearly warranted. Aside from John's reaction, I was even more determined. I knew as soon as he walked back to the bedroom, at that point, today I was going to have to face this situation alone and it was just me against the world.

The day started out like any other had over the past ten years, getting my uniform on and getting chow and going to work. Unbe-knownst to me, this day would turn out to end like no other in my life before. As I drove onto base, John and I had a heated discussion in the car. He was upset with me and I at the same time felt power-less to try to get him to support me in this decision. After dropping him off at his unit on base, I headed over to the chow hall and I put our argument behind me as I started thinking of what I had to do today. I figured I would just have to deal later with the fallout of coming out and how it would affect our relationship. One thing I was thinking about was I needed to come up with an excuse to tell the Gunnery Sergeant about the extended lunch I would need to take that day. The reporter from ABC World Evening News would be expecting me, off base at lunchtime to do the interview.

I drove over to the Chow Hall that morning, got out and walked in. I wondered if I would be able to do this next week when everyone would know who I was. To avoid the hassle of dealing with the other Marines and their attitudes, I was already planning on never eating at the Chow Hall again.

After eating breakfast I headed to my unit, Marine Corps Base Food Service Office, where I worked in Supply. It was a long morning and going through my mind the whole time was that the Marines could not find out what I was about ready to do before I did it. My heart was racing as I was afraid that they would foil my plans and that would end my goal to make a lasting difference before getting out of the Corps. I worried that if they found out what I was about ready to do then someone high up in the Marine Corps would call ABC News and get the interview canceled.

I had seen examples of how the Marine Corps had gone to lengths in the past to protect its image and from my experiences with the Naval Criminal Investigative Services (NCIS) it made me a bit paranoid. The military and NCIS have a history of tracking gay servicemembers and ruining their lives. Because of the clandestine way the military seeks out gay servicemembers, one learns to not trust people in general, to lie, and to strategize to survive in a hostile environment. Over the years, I had learned how to ride that fine line and to be as out as I could without getting caught. I had come to loathe the hypocrisy and the witchhunts in the Marines and the Navy that destroyed so many of my friends' lives. I wanted to throw it back in their faces and stand up and fight the injustice that I had seen throughout my ten years in the Corps.

The Marine Corps is a close fraternity and goes to lengths to protect its reputation and would not want one of their own, in their words, "embarrassing" the Corps. Up until now no Marine had come out publicly or nationally, like other service members had done from the Army, Navy, and Air Force. The Commandant of the Marine Corps, Carl Mundy, with swagger, even made a comment to the sort that gays in the military was not an issue for the Marines as there were no gays in the Marine Corps. Well, I was about ready to change all that.

Sitting at work that morning, I didn't get anything accomplished. I was about to explode with adrenaline. I kept looking at my watch waiting for 1130 hours to roll around so that I could go meet the ABC News reporter. I had butterflies in my stomach and racing through my mind was the same thought over and over again, "please doesn't let the Marines find out before I do this". At this point in my mind and spirit I was determined to complete this mission and nothing was going to stop me; not John, friends, parents, or the Marine Corps.

At lunch I told the gunny that I would be back a bit late from lunch as I had some bills to take care of. My heart was pounding so hard I wondered if anybody noticed when I left. Would this be the last time I would have to lie to them to play within their rules? I was already in the uniform that I needed to wear, so I drove off base to the hotel on the edge of Jacksonville where I was to do the interview.

I still remember the day like it was yesterday. The wind was blowing and it was chilly outside. The sun was brightly shining, almost in a way laughing a me, like everything was okay. It seemed to be making a mockery of the seriousness and the stress of the moment. As I got out of my car and walked toward the entrance to the hotel, I could already feel my life changing. My stomach was in knots and I was on an adrenaline high. As I entered the hotel, one of my first thoughts was, I hope the hotel desk clerk doesn't call the Marines and tell them that there is this Marine being interviewed in one of the hotel rooms and it looks suspicious.

I walked up to the counter and asked for the reporter and

what room they were in. The reporter came downstairs and met me in the lobby. As we walked upstairs and into the hotel room, I suddenly had the feeling of being led to the gallows. Upon coming into the hotel room, there were black umbrellas, the kind that photographers use, placed all over the room. The TV was turned on and tuned to ABC and the coverage of the day's events, which was President Clinton meeting with the Joint Chiefs of Staff and them wrangling over what the outcome on the ban on gays in the military should be. I was surprised by the TV being on, as I didn't know how that was going to figure into the interview. As it turned out, the ABC news crew wanted to get some shots of me watching the coverage and then interviewing me on my reactions to the final decision and why was I coming out right now. The newsman started asking me some pre-interview questions and we talked about what he was going to ask me on air. I was sweating like a horse and was very anxious about Clinton announcing that they would get rid of the policy. I had written some notes on a 3 x 5 card as to what I would say. I knew by this time that the sound bite would be important and I wanted the right message to come across. As I sat there the decision I had made hit me hard and I started thinking of how I had gotten to this point, to put my career in jeopardy after so long in the Marines. It's times like these, that you really sit back and reflect and you ask yourself, how did I end up here and where did it all start?

As I sat there watching the TV, my heart began to sink as it became clear that Clinton was not going to overturn the policy. I sat there in shock as I watched him announce the six-month interim policy. Holy Shit! What would happen to me now? I suddenly had a sinking and ominous feeling and was totally disgusted with how he had just thrown all of us gay and lesbian servicemembers under the bus. The reporter then asked me if I still wanted to go through with the decision to come out and I said "yes." I had made the decision and had come this far and I wanted to make a difference, even if the President had blinked. I was going to stand up for what was morally and ethically right and try to change the Corps for the better. Now was my moment and when it came time I wanted to make sure I said the right thing. I was not going to back down now. I had a mission to accomplish and I was ready to walk over the divide.

As soon as the cameras started to roll they asked me some questions and I answered them. My palms were sweaty and I had this ball in my throat that kept creeping up, threatening to cut off my air supply. But I knew what I had to do and nothing was going to stop me. All of my life experiences had prepared me for this moment and I was calling on all of them at that moment to come out to the nation.

After the interview the enormity of what I had done hadn't sunk in yet as I drove back on base. As soon as I walked into my unit my Gunnery Sergeant stopped me right in the middle of the office within earshot of everyone in the office and said "I just got a call from Cheryl with the Montel Williams show and she was looking for you." My stomach dropped to my knees and my mind was racing to come up with a quick response as there was no way the Marines could find out before I appeared that evening on the news.

I immediately said that she was a friend of my sister and that I knew her. This was another lie on top of others that I had been putting out there for the past ten years. When would it stop? Thank goodness he bought the story hook, line and sinker, or at least I hoped he had. But I knew in the back of my mind that come tonight they all would know the whole truth and everyone that had known me for the past ten years in the Marine Corps would be going back and looking at their relationship with me to include the Marines I currently worked with. What would they think now? I couldn't think about this, I had to stay strong and look forward and not look back or second guess what I was doing.

The end of the day couldn't come quick enough and my adrenalin was going strong as I walked out of my unit and drove off base to the house to change and go to the gay bar, Friends Lounge, to watch the evening news. I didn't have to pick up John as a mutual friend of ours, a Navy Corpsman, was going to take him home. On the way home I was on cloud nine as it hit me what I had just done. No matter what they did to me now or what happened I had a BIG weight off of my chest.

I turned the radio up on the way home and enjoyed the moment. I was finally free with no secrets. I knew what I had done was the right thing as I felt it in my spirit. John wasn't at the house when I stopped to change clothes which I was happy about as I didn't want to have to deal with any negativity at this point. I needed to look ahead and stay positive. I felt like I really needed to call a few of my military veteran friends for some advice on what to do next. So I called Alan Stephens, Joe Granger and Tanya Domi. Tanya was a former Army Captain, now with the National Gay and Lesbian Task Force, (NGLTF) and a close friend. When I talked to her, she recommended that I call my Warrant Officer as a courtesy and explain to him what I had done to give him a heads-up.

I did not want to do this, as I would have to face someone who I knew would be hostile to me and pissed off at what I had done. I would later find out that of all the people I dealt with in the following days my Warrant Officer would turn out to be the one to watch out for. I picked up the phone and dialed his phone number. He answered and I immediately told him that I had to tell him something. I started in and said that I did an interview today with ABC World Evening News telling them I was gay and that I wanted to give him a heads-up to the interview that would air nationally in about an hour on ABC. At this point I heard silence as I stood there imagining what the look on his face was. He then proceeded to thank me for letting him know and that he didn't subscribe to some of the talk in the office recently, in which one of the Marines had said "all gays should be shot."

After the phone call I sat down and made a couple more calls to friends. I then changed and left the house for the bar to watch the evening news with my other gay friends.

Once I got to Friends Lounge I was the only one there along with the bartender and a couple of other gay civilians. There was a couch set up in one corner of the bar with the TV on.

As it got closer to the time for the piece to show more people arrived and found out what I had done. Everyone was positive but I could see the concern on their faces. When the piece finally came on I watched as they played the decision of Clinton caving into the Joint Chiefs and setting out a six-month review under what would eventually be called "Don't Ask, Don't Tell" (DADT).

They then played my interview as a reaction to Clinton's decision. They only played one sentence from the interview, which was, "I just couldn't stand by and not say a thing, I mean we got to stand up and say hey there are thousands of us out there and you know, this discrimination is wrong." I felt at that moment watching my coming out on national television, as if I was standing up for every Marine that had been discharged from the military for being gay or lesbian and I was calling the Marine Corps out on their discrimination. I felt vindication, empowerment and at the same time apprehension deep down that I had broken a big rule by coming out to the Marines. But I did it because I wanted to change the rules.

I left the bar afterwards and drove back to the house worried as I knew I would have to face John and his wrath. When I came in the door John was furious with me. He proceeded to tell me that there were two messages on the answering machine for me. One was from someone at the Pentagon but was cut off. The second message was one that was ominous and portrayed what was to come. Upon listening to the machine I heard a sizzling sound. Somewhere someone had held the phone receiver over a frying pan and you could hear the oil crackling obviously inferring that

I would burn for what I had done. That was it. That evening I had to deal with the decision which I knew was right and at the same time try to explain to John why I did it. He went to bed and left me standing there alone. That feeling of being alone was rough. At that moment I felt it was just me against the world.

I thought if I got this type of reaction from John who was close to me, what would be the reaction of everyone else? I had no idea of what was to come, but that day set in motion events that would change my life forever, challenge me beyond belief and push my limits to the brink before the next four years were over.

CHAPTER 2
EARLY LESSONS

0310 hours 7 July 1962 Cheyenne, Wyoming

I was born in the early morning hours on July 7, 1962 at DePaul Catholic Hospital in Cheyenne, Wyoming. My father was in the Air Force stationed at F.E. Warren Air Force Base on the outskirts of Cheyenne. My mother was a housewife. A short time after I was born my parents decided to move to a farm thirty miles east of Cheyenne near the farming communities of Carpenter and Burns. On our farm we mainly raised horses and hogs. My father was an excellent horse trainer and the farm allowed him to have quite a few horses.

Some of my earliest memories growing up on the farm in those early years were of watching Captain Kangaroo, Lost in Space, and Star Trek on television, and playing out in the pastures of our farm. While growing up I loved my Lincoln Logs, planes and had a fascination for things that flew. One morning, during the summer of '69, my mother called me into the living room while I was eating breakfast. This was the day where my interest in space and planes took off. As I sat there on the living room floor eating my corn flakes, I watched on our black and white television the fuzzy picture of Neil Armstrong walking down the ladder and stepping on the surface of the moon. Walter Cronkite was narrating what was going on. At that moment, I felt a hunger and fascination for learning more about space, and astronauts.

After this day I would tell those around me that I wanted to be an astronaut when I grew up. This spurred my interest in my favorite television programs Lost in Space and Star Trek and anything science fiction when I was young. My parents would later buy me a telescope and I spent nights out on the front sidewalk looking at the craters on the moon. Because there is no light pollution from cities out west on the prairie, you can look up at the sky at night and see thousands of stars in the Milky Way. This is one of the things that I miss most from living out on the farm as a boy.

In those early years my father and mother instilled in me a sense of responsibility and respect for life, and for rules. Sometimes that lesson came hard. Before I was even in kindergarten I would help my father on the farm taking care of the animals, building barns and corrals. One day when I was around five, I was with my father at a neighbor's farm helping build a corral for their cattle. While playing in the corral, I came across a grey tabby kitten and I thought it would be cool to see him swim. I proceeded to put him in the stock tank where the cattle drank and took a stick and kept poking him under the water so that I could see him swim underwater. At some point to my disappointment he stopped moving and he drowned. That was the day I found out that barn animals don't breathe underwater. As soon as my father found out about the kitten he left welts on my legs that day by way of his belt and lesson learned.

Besides playing on the farm and helping my father, I have very few memories of anything else before kindergarten. However, when I entered kindergarten I was suddenly thrust into the harsh environment of dealing with other kids. On my first day of school I was so short that I had to put my books on the first step of the bus and use both of my hands to pull myself up the three steps to get into the bus. For some reason the bus driver thought this was funny and made a few sarcastic remarks. He continued to tease me for various reasons throughout grade school. This of course just gave the other kids a reason to do the same. This was the beginning of my getting bullied by others in my youth.

My kindergarten memories are filled with colorful paints and the big paint brushes that we had, Play-Doh, learning how to write, my multicolored rug I slept on for our nap time, and of course getting in trouble for talking during our nap time. One day during our afternoon nap time when we were supposed to be sleeping on our rugs, I was caught talking to one of the other boys. I found out that besides sitting on a hot car seat in the summer that a ping pong paddle can also warm up your seat and sting. Lesson learned was that you shouldn't talk during nap time! I obeyed the rules after that and never got paddled in kindergarten again.

Throughout grade school I really liked English, Music and Acting. When Christmas time came around I was an angel in the school play. I had a silver halo made with a coat hanger and tinsel wrapped around it from our Christmas tree. Christmas has always been my favorite holiday and my favorite Christmas story when I was a kid was Rudolph the Red-Nose Reindeer. Playing an angel in the Christmas play was certainly better than playing the turkey for the Thanksgiving play when I was in the cub scouts. I really hated getting picked to be the turkey. I had to wear long johns and I looked like a plucked turkey. Not soon after that I quit the cub scouts. I really didn't fit in. Even then in those early years I knew I was different, if only because the other kids let me know it.

Recesses in grade school were difficult and the kids were mean. Many times I ended up making up my own games and stuck to myself. As a matter of fact, because we lived so far out in the country with no other kids around after school, I escaped into books as a boy until my little sister got bigger and I had someone to play with.

Reading was my way of escaping the trials and tribulations of growing up. One of my favorite books as a boy was Where The Red Fern Grows, which is about a boy and his dogs. It is also about overcoming adversity. I have always had a fascination for books or movies about people overcoming adversity.

Around this same time I had a Basset Hound named Cloe. One night as my father was backing up the truck in the back yard, he by accident ran over Cloe. I was devastated, especially when he told me that she needed to be put down. That meant that my father was going to use the shotgun to put her out of her misery. The night that he shot her I cried myself to sleep and felt an emptiness not having my best friend around anymore. This was pretty traumatic for me as a boy, losing my best friend, at the same time learning a hard lesson about life and death.

Around third grade my parents moved me from Carpenter Elementary School to Hillsdale Elementary School, which was about fifteen miles away, because of the effect the bullying in school was having on me. I was unhappy and my grades were reflecting the stress of what I was going through. Fourth grade proved to be a pivotal time in my life. My teacher, Miss Wallace, was like a mother to me in a lot of ways. She was stern when she needed to be but was also very loving and accepting.

During fourth grade we also had another teacher working as an intern with Miss Wallace. His name was Mr. Smiley. It was during this time that I had my first real teacher's crush and it was on Mr. Smiley. At the time nothing seemed unusual to me about it, however, looking back on it years later as I was coming out I realized it was one of those key markers in my life. I just liked spending time being around Mr. Smiley. However, it didn't last forever as Mr. Smiley was scheduled to leave us around Christmas time. I was depressed about it when I found out and I didn't get to say goodbye to him because when he was getting ready to leave I had the chicken pox. This was right around the Christmas pageant and so I missed the Christmas play and saying goodbye to Mr. Smiley. My sadness over Mr. Smiley leaving was something at the time I couldn't express or understand. I cried when he left because I missed him.

I started learning about sex around the fourth grade. Throughout grade school I had fooled around with some of the boys in my classes. Fooling around with guys consisted of a bit more than show and tell. This continued until junior high, when I started fooling around with a couple of upperclassmen. It was fun and seemed very natural to me. I really don't remember much of wanting to hang around the girls at the time.

When I was growing up I was attracted to the cute guys in grade school and high school and always tried to find a way to hang around them and make friends and then eventually fool around with them. When I did, it was always consensual.

My first time seeing an adult male naked was at the military base swimming pool when I was in grade school. Total fascination reigned as I stood there in the pool locker room and stared at the naked men and the large penises. There was a desire, which I couldn't express or understand at the time. I had this fascination and yearning of wanting to watch and be around men. Years later when I was coming out I looked back on these things and it helped me to come to grips with accepting myself and realizing that I had been born this way.

Both fifth and sixth grades were a blur. However, I remember the transition from sixth grade to junior high being significant, as this was when I started having interactions with high school students and I went through puberty. Now I had to start dealing with older kids and deal with the pressures of being a teenager. From kindergarten to sixth grade I was generally a naïve kid who could never understand why I didn't fit in.

It was around seventh grade when I realized in order to fit in I would need to have a girlfriend. It was a status thing and I realized to play by society's rules that I had to find one. As I was going through this I was still fooling around with the boys at the same time, which didn't seem odd to me. I only fooled around with one girl at the time and my father found out about it. I used to play spin the bottle in the back of the bus and behind the school house with

20

this one particular girl, named Julie. It was always innocent show and tell, that was until a high school student named Chuck found out about it and decided it would be funny to tell my father. I was horrified because he told my father about it as I was standing there. My father and I were at a neighbor's farm one afternoon. Just as we were getting ready to leave, Chuck, who had found out about me fooling around with Julie, told me that he was going to tell my father. As we were getting ready to leave and getting into the truck, Chuck ran up to the truck window and with glee announced what I had done to my father as I was standing there. I just wanted to die at that moment. As we drove out of the farm my father was silent in the truck until we got out on the highway. I thought my father was going to beat me. This was when my father was being really hard on my sister and I. When my father spoke he asked me what had happened and told me that he was not upset. He then proceeded to share his own experiences about fooling around with girls. I felt relieved but at the same time I found it somewhat perverse to be talking with my father about sex. I really couldn't envision my father having sex with my mother or anyone else and because my feelings for guys was stronger by then, I still felt a divide between us.

At the time I felt my father was trying to relate to me. It was one of the first moments that I can remember in my life where my father tried to bond with me man-to-man. It was like there was an understanding between two men about the way life was. At that moment I really wish I could have told my father about my feelings for guys, but I knew that would be going too far. At some shallow level we bonded, but the secret of my true desires never came out. When we got home he gave me a book about the "birds and the bees" from a Christian viewpoint and that was it. It was never discussed again. I don't think he ever told my mother because she never mentioned it. It was something only a father and son would share. Because I was fooling around with guys, my fellow classmates, I was worried that someone would find out and tell my parents about it. At the end of the day there wasn't anything in that book about the "birds and the bees" that explained having sex with guys. Somehow that was left out, so I started on a quest to find books or anything that would give me a perspective on these feelings I had toward other guys.

My parents were pretty strict while we were growing up. They fought sometimes like couples do and those were the times when we hid. It bothered me and I didn't want to be around my father when he got mad. When they did fight my mother usually won. The way I saw it as I was growing up was that my mother was manipulative and always got her way. The earliest memories of my father are of an authoritarian. I was scared of my father growing up and I also eventually came to avoid any close relationship with my mother. As I got older I continued to grow further apart from them. My parents became more religious as they got older; at the same time I was discovering that I was attracted to guys. I found out these two things were in conflict according to my parents and the fundamentalist church we went to.

When I was young we went to a Methodist Church but as I got into junior and senior high we started attending an Assemblies of God Pentecostal church in Pines Bluff, Wyoming, which was a neighboring farming community about twenty miles away. Most Sunday mornings started out with us watching Jimmy Swaggart or the PTL Club with Jim and Tammy Faye Baker on television during breakfast and then going to Sunday school and church.

Sunday evenings were spent going to a Revival Pentecostal church service. During these Sunday evening church services there was "speaking in tongues" and listening to sermons about "hell fire" and "brimstone." It was during this time that my internal clock was in total disarray as I heard one thing from the church and my parents, but deep down inside of me I felt something totally different. I hid this from everyone. I had kids at school calling me a "fag," which I hid from my parents for good reason. Adding insult to injury, I would then come home to my parents and to our Church, both of whom vilified gays and lesbians. Throughout High School, at every one of these church services, I used to pray to Jesus to take away this desire for guys away from me, but that never happened no matter how hard I prayed.

My father went through a period where he was really abusive to us kids, and my sister in particular got the worst of the treatment. My sister hated the taste of milk. One day when my sister was gagging on her milk at the dinner table my father grabbed her by her hair and yanked her away from the table and then proceeded to beat her. He went on to punish her with his belt so badly that the next day at school her gym teacher saw the bleeding welts on her back and reported my parents. Nothing happened to them and they felt they were the victims throughout the whole situation.

My mother got mad at my sister and blamed her because of this. Even though my father chilled out as we got older, I was never able to develop a trusting relationship with my parents so that I could tell them how I felt or what was really going on in my life. That's not to say we didn't do things together as a family when we were growing up, like going camping and going to the drive-in theater, but it was always overshadowed by my father's and mother's authoritarian ways. As my parents became more religious, we stopped doing things as a family that my parents saw as evil or against Christianity, like going to see movies or any event where alcohol was present.

My sister was a year and a half younger than me, and my brother six years younger. Because my sister was so close to me in age we were almost like twins. We lived so far out in the country with no other farms close to us so I played with my sister at home. We played Cowboys and Indians a lot and acted out TV shows that we saw. I used to wear a sheet and pretend it was a cape and jump off the huge haystacks on the farm like I was Batman.

We used to play long into the afternoons, and then, when it started getting dark, mother would call us in for dinner to wash up, eat, watch a little bit of TV and then go to bed and hopefully fall asleep before our father got home. Those nights coming in from playing and getting to watch movies like Ben Hur or The Wizard of Oz were some of my favorite memories during those summers. One day during the summer when I was eleven years old, my sister and I were playing out in the pasture. Mother called for us to come in. When we came in my mother accused us of fooling around, playing doctor and doing show and tell. Nothing of which could have been further from the truth. We tried to explain to our mother that we had done nothing of the sort but she didn't believe my sister or I. There was nothing that should have caused my mother not to believe us as we were not habitual liars as kids.

For punishment, she had us take off all of our clothes and had us stand across from one another for about a half an hour, naked. This was a traumatic experience for me at the time since I was standing naked across from my sister and she the same across from me. I still to this day have never forgiven my mother for this incident because she never believed us when we were telling the truth. I am embarrassed even writing about this, but think it is important that parents treat their children right. It was one of the situations growing up that pushed me further away from my mother. When I got into junior high, my mother got even stranger. One day I went to hug her and she said it wasn't natural anymore since I was getting older. I was taken aback from the experience and rarely hugged my mother after that.

CHAPTER 3
DISCOVERY

0800 hours 16 September 1976 Burns, Wyoming

I started junior high on September, 16 1976. I began to realize during seventh and eighth grade that life and societal rules were changing. Fooling around with girls and having a girlfriend was the rule of thumb, but fooling around with the guys was not part of the rules and I needed to keep it to myself. Up until now I had fooled around with a few of my classmates and one of my cousins and I enjoyed it.

In junior high something changed though, because the boys didn't want to fool around anymore and wanted to hang around the girls instead. I wanted to continue to hang out with the boys and I didn't care for the girls at all. I couldn't figure it out. I still liked the boys but they now liked the girls. I found out that the difference was connected to the words "gay" or "fag," which was what the older high school students were calling me. This was when I really noticed that I was different. It was like a fork in the road and I was taking one path and the other boys were taking a different one.

I felt this loneliness that I was different, and realization set in that this was something that I should not tell anyone, especially my parents. I had enough self-esteem to stick up for myself, but I didn't have enough at the time to be able to intimidate the other guys because of this secret. Sometimes it seemed like the older high school students could look at me, read right through me and see that I was gay. I knew down deep inside that they were right.

I tried as hard as I could to mask myself and play by their

rules. At that age I was trying to explore and discover what "gay" was, and at the same time trying to pray it away. One night around this time, ABC television was doing a special on the music group, the Village People. The announcer was talking about the controversy surrounding the group, and about them being gay. I was sitting in the living room at the time with my mother. As I sat there watching the television I was immediately engaged in wondering what this group was all about. I had to be careful though because I couldn't let on to my mother that I was interested. I was sitting there trying not to act to interested in front of her, but at the same time listening intently.

My mother started to disparage the performers on television and said that what they were was an abomination of God and that these guys were going to go to hell. As I listened to my mother say this I was self identifying with these guys and I felt a kinship with them. I wanted to know more and I knew I was just like them. This just re-enforced my belief that I couldn't tell my parents about what was being said about me at school or how I really felt down deep inside.

It was around this same time that I started noticing that I was attracted to certain actors on television as well. I thought that Robert Conrad from the Wild Wild West show was hot and loved it every time he took off his shirt. The same goes for the show Trapper John, M.D. Every time Gregory Harrison took off his shirt and showed his hairy chest in the beginning credits of the show something always twitched inside of me and I knew that I was really attracted to that. I felt an attraction that I couldn't put into words.

In junior and senior high school my school days started out by eating scrambled eggs, running down the driveway to the bus, a thirty-minute ride to school, and getting to my locker and my classes on time. After school I usually stayed for band practice or wrestling practice.

I hated the bus and the hallways at school because these

were the places that I tried to avoid the bullies, the upperclass-men. When I was in junior high there was one bully who always screwed with me on the bus. One day I was fed up. He got on the bus and smacked me on his way to the back of the bus. I got up, set my books down, yelled at him and as he turned around I threw a punch and hit him square in the face giving him a black eye. He never touched me again.

The bullies at school were untouchable because they had free reign and could do whatever they wanted to others and not get in trouble with the staff at school. The teachers and the staff just turned a blind eye to what certain bullies did. What they did was accepted as an initiation. One time when I was in the hallway at school I started defending myself against this upperclassman named Larry. The coach at the time saw the whole incident and then proceeded to tell me that I couldn't defend myself and that I needed to shut up. He was an enabler for the bullies in the school. He was a young insecure coach who tried to be just one of the guys. He laughed and joked when the seniors beat up and hazed the other students. This moment with the coach and the bully was an epiphany for me. Here I was following what my father said to do, which was fight back, and here I had a teacher telling me I shouldn't fight back and to shut up and take it. This didn't sit well with me and just made me that much more determined to stand up to the anti-gay bullying.

Telling the world that I got picked on as a kid and teen is hard for me to do, as I am really not proud of this and am quite embar-rassed. I wasn't weak, just sensitive, nice and naïve. This bullying throughout grade school, junior and senior high, shaped my view of life and how to handle relationships and it really affected me once I realized I was not like everyone else and that I was gay. As I look back on it now, going through this adversity in my youth helped me later on deal with what I would have to face in the Ma-rine Corps.

As I tried to fit in, I tried to get involved with the extracurricular activities that I liked, one of which was music. In grade school I had started playing a woodwind instrument that would lead me to playing the clarinet in the school orchestra and marching band.

I did well in Band, and began to expand my skills and started playing the bass clarinet, tenor and baritone saxophones. I also decided to try out for the school choir, and to my teachers' amazement I did really well. So much so that one day while I was still in junior high, the choir teacher called me into the high school students choir practice and had me sing for them. I went onto audition for the Wyoming All State Choir. I made it, and got to make the trip to Rawlins, Wyoming for All State.

I used to watch entertainment shows on television where there were singers and dancers and I wished my high school would have had dance because I know I would have done well. A couple of years after graduating high school I saw the television show "Fame," a musical drama series about a New York City High School for the performing arts. I really wished my life would have been different and I could have gone to a school like that.

Instead, Burns High School, which I was attending, only had band and choir. It was a small country school. There were only 30 people in my graduating class. I had never heard of Broadway or show tunes when I was in high school but if I had I am sure I would have liked them. I lived a sheltered life growing up in a small farming community.

I also got involved in sports in high school. I had participated in little league as a kid and loved baseball and softball. I still cherish those early memories of my father playing catch with me helping me with my throwing and catching. My father really wanted me to excel at it. My mother and father encouraged me to get involved in sports early on. My mother in particular was not the type to be worried about a sport being too dangerous. My mother used to tell me that I was too sensitive. I did not have the stereotypically coddling mother. I think it was because she suspected I was gay.

My high school was so small that we only had four sports. Football, which I was too small for, basketball which I was too short for, track, which really didn't interest me and then wrestling. I had a short stocky build and so I wrestled for four years in high school but never really excelled at it like others did. I did get a chance, when I was a senior, to start taking judo lessons outside of school. It was a sport that I was really good at and my school didn't have.

My father had started first, as he was taking judo lessons as part of a class at the Laramie County Community College in Cheyenne, Wyoming. I went to watch one of his classes one day and I immediately wanted to try the sport. I started taking lessons and I loved it. A husband and wife team that taught judo as a part of a club. At some point my father quit and refused to let me continue. The instructors saw promise in me continuing the sport and tried to talk my parents into letting me continue, but they wouldn't.

We also went to rodeos when I was growing up and I wanted to do barrel racing. I found out, however, that barrel racing was considered a girls rodeo sport, so I never got into the rodeo circuit like my brother did. I could never understand, and still don't, why barrel racing on the straight rodeo circuit is considered only a women's sport. On the gay rodeo circuit, which is big in the United States, men compete in barrel racing. If judo, softball, soccer and volleyball (all sports I later played in the Marines and did very well at) would have been offered at my high school, I would have played those sports.

I think the reason that I excelled in judo and other sports outside of high school was that they were in a supportive environment. I did not have that supportive environment in high school when it came to sports, especially during physical education, "PE." When I was in junior high and high school we had PE with the upperclassmen. PE ended up being a nightmare for me and other kids who got bullied in school because some of the older high school students used dodge ball as a game of bullying to see how big of a welt they could leave.

The locker room after PE was the worst place, as it was out of the prying eyes of the coach and staff even though they turned a blind eye to the bullying. The upperclassmen played a game of putting the underclassman into these small lockers and closing them and leaving them in there for extended periods of time. I had this only happen to me once. I have claustrophobia, so thank God they didn't leave me in there that long.

But the worst experience I ever had in the school locker rooms came one afternoon when I was a freshman. I was in the locker room finishing up getting dressed after PE. I was the last one in the lockerroom along with a senior named Greg. He was tall and good-looking, dark haired and hairy from head to toe. He was in the shower toweling off in the doorway that leads from the showers to the lockers. I was across the way standing at my locker. I turned around and saw him and he started talking to me. In the course of the conversation he asked me if I liked what I saw and then he asked me if I wanted to fool around. Now up to this point I had fooled around with a couple of upperclassman and it was always consensual. So I thought here was another upperclassman who I thought was hot, coming onto me. I told him yes. He immediately turned on me and said he was only joking and he was going to tell everyone what I said.

I had just been gay baited, and I was scared as hell. After getting dressed he proceeded to go and tell the coach and a good number of the high school students in the school. I wanted to just die at this point, and I was scared my parents were going to find out. Years later looking back on this incident, I realized that men who gay bait or gay bash someone are usually closet cases themselves and do so to cover up their own repressed homosexuality.

Another way that I tried to fit during junior and senior high was in academics and clubs. During my junior and senior years I consistently made the honor rolls and had a consistent high grade point average. I excelled in Music, Civics, English and Journalism. During my senior year I wrote and put together an article in our local high school paper on the upcoming presidential election. I later received a Wyoming High School State Journalism award for the article.

I also got involved in 4H. Unlike my younger brother who got involved in Future Farmers of America (FFA) and raised hogs, I got involved in 4H and raised rabbits for food and showed them at the county fair. I also started a bible club in my high school.

Even though I was involved in these extracurricular activities I still didn't fit in. I started thinking that I needed a girlfriend as a status symbol to fit in, so I set out to find one.

Now when it came to finding a girlfriend that was not easy either as I was not a popular kid in school or part of any clique. I was a loner but an outgoing kid. Nor was I the only outcast in our class. There were the girls who were too fat, the poor kid who always stunk, the girl who had really bad zits and the guys who liked Dungeons and Dragons, and computers in general. I eventually dated a couple of girls from within this group that didn't fit in with what society called popular. For me, sex was not a part of this dating experience. It was strictly platonic. I had no desire to have sex with a girl and wouldn't have felt comfortable as it is. I was dating these girls as friends because I thought that was what I needed to do to fit in. I eventually realized that dating these girls didn't change my social status or make me any more popular.

Around this same time I met Jack, who would become my best friend throughout high school. He was about six-feet tall, had black hair, was geeky, eccentric and a Mormon. He had a thing for Neil Sedaka, oldies music, and computers. He definitely came across as different, and like me, was also called a fag at school.

Jack however, was different in that he took it all in stride and never let being called a fag bother him. To this day I admire how he just shrugged off being called a fag and marched to his own drum. Jack was one of those key people in my life who helped me realize that you should be yourself.

Spending time with Jack in a way was liberating because it made me not care as much about what people thought. At some point I started accepting my own differences, even if it was as small as not trying to fit in anymore. The first time my parents met Jack, I got a stern look from my mother. I instinctively knew right away why I got that look, but I played stupid. Later on my parents sat me down and explained to me that Jack was gay.

My father sitting there in our living room asked me if I knew what "gay" was. I said I thought so and he said, "well, it is guys who like to suck dicks." Hell I knew that, but I had to be careful about what I said in front of my parents. They couldn't find out that I was fooling around with guys.

They forbade me to stop hanging around Jack. I was pissed off and in shock. He was my best friend and they wanted me to stay away from him. This was a pivotal point in my life, as I really never disobeyed my parents. I had always followed the rules. I didn't drink or do drugs, I went to church and I followed what my parents, teachers and pastor at church always said to do. But there was no way that I was going to stop hanging around my only friend in high school. Jack was the only guy in my class who really was not an asshole, and he was a good person. Jack's friendship was unconditional and I was not going to treat a good friend like shit. I continued to hang out with Jack; I just didn't let my parents know about it.

This however was not the first time that my parents had pointed out that something that I was doing was not considered in their view "normal." I think my parents realized I was different as a kid and teen and encouraged me to walk, talk and act in a way that they saw that men in our society should behave.

Throughout grade school, junior and senior high school I was constantly hearing from my father and mother, "that is for girls, boys don't do that." For example, when I was learning how to play catch, my father would often point out that the way I started throwing the baseball was the way girls threw. When I got into junior and senior high, I had so many books at the time that I would sometimes carry them in front of me, holding them to my chest. My father noticed this and angrily pointed out that guys carried their books by their side. I quickly changed the way I carried my books because I didn't want people to think I was gay.

I eventually found my way in high school and accepted the fact that I was not going to be liked by everyone. I was really in the wrong environment and the wrong school for a young gay kid. Being gay in the eighties was not a positive thing to those around me in Wyoming. As I got closer to graduation, I could hardly wait to get out of high school and leave Wyoming and never look back.

I did not want to stay in Wyoming and stay with the same people I had just graduated with who really couldn't care less about me. I wanted to get away and explore the world. I was not going to go with them to the University of Wyoming or the local Community College. I decided to go to Northwest Bible College outside of Seattle, Washington for a Music degree.

In September of 1980 I found myself one night at the Greyhound bus station in Cheyenne with my bags packed as my parents were about to see me off to Seattle to college. As I was sitting there I looked across the way at this really cute guy who was reading a book. It was a Gordon Merrick book and had two guys kissing on the front of it. I instinctively knew it was a gay romance novel as I had seen them before at the local cigar shop in Cheyenne. While I was looking at the guy he looked over and we both smiled at one another and in that instant there was an acknowledgement and understanding of something we had in common. I really wanted to say something to this guy but I couldn't because my parents

33

were right there. Soon I would be out of the authoritarian clutches of my parents. Then I could really find out what being gay was all about. The next day I made it to Seattle to embark on my college experience.

CHAPTER 4
ESCAPE

0800 hours 25 August 1980 Kirkland, Washington

I started my first day of Northwest Bible College on August 25, 1980. I quickly made friends. One of my first roommates was Kel Stiles who I got along great with. After some initial discussions and probing about our personal lives, I came to find out that Kel was also gay and had the same "temptations."

Like Jack in high school, Kel turned out to be another key friend in my life in helping me discover who I was which led to my eventual acceptance of myself. Meeting Kel and other guys in bible college who had these same desires as I had was an eye-opening experience. We all constantly prayed for it to be taken away, and at the same time supported one another. Because God didn't take this away from us, I started questioning the fundamentalist Christian view of homosexuality.

During that first year of college, Kel and I got involved in volunteering and doing some street ministry in downtown Seattle. Once a week we would go downtown to Pike Street Market and minister to the homeless and the prostitutes. I was really surprised and excited by what I discovered going into the big city and talking to folks. Being from a farm this was my first big city experience. There was one particular person who was a male prostitute that we talked to.

At one point we talked him into coming back to campus so that we could pray with him. How funny it is to look back on this now and think how we were trying to save him, but we were the ones that needed help! I was really kind of intrigued by the whole situation. I was scared to look in the guy's eyes, figuring he would know that I was gay. I realized early on that sometimes just by looking at someone's eyes I could tell if they were gay. Some people really bear their souls and personalities through their eyes. We of course didn't save this guy's soul and I think we all ended up more frustrated than he was.

While in high school and college I had this guilt that I had taken on by listening to my parents and the church. It really was weighing on me, and I was often depressed because God would not take these feelings away no matter how hard I prayed.

While in college, I was too young to go to bars, but I found out about a gay bathhouse in downtown Seattle and decided to go check it out. This was my first sexual experience with guys since high school. I continued to be on the fence at fighting this urge but at the same time exploring it as I came to the end of my first year in college.

Ultimately, I didn't have enough money to go to a second year of college, so I said goodbye to Kel and my other friends in Seattle and headed back to Wyoming.

When I got back to Cheyenne, I stayed with my parents to save money while I worked two jobs. I finally had gotten to a point where I wanted to tell my mother that I thought I was gay. So one afternoon as she was standing in the kitchen cooking, I decided that I would tell her. The conversation started out with me telling her about something in my life that I had been fighting and that I was coming to a realization about it. I just blurted it out to her that I thought I was gay and waited for her reaction.

For a minute there was silence and then she asked why I thought I was gay. I proceeded to tell her about the feelings and that I had prayed for God to take them away but he hadn't, so I felt that I was always going to be this way and I was accepting it. She didn't cry or seem shocked. Instead, she told me that I was going to go to hell if I stayed with what she called "the gay lifestyle," and that I should get help. I asked her not to tell my father and to please keep it between us. At the time I was still scared of my father and his temper.

Later that afternoon, after my father came home, I was outside and my parents called me in the house and by the look on my father's face I knew what had happened. My mother had told my father after I had asked her not to. This really was the last straw that ruined any remaining trust I had with my mother.

I really felt she had betrayed my trust after I had shared something so personal with her. My father and mother wanted to send me to a psychologist to get help. I told them no. At this point they told me I would have to get out of the house if I wasn't going to try to get psychological help. Down deep inside of me I knew there was nothing wrong with me. There was no way I was going to go to a psychologist, so I immediately got an apartment the next day in Cheyenne and moved out. This incident forced me to make a choice on the road to accepting myself for who I was instead of taking on the guilt of being gay that my parents and society were laying on me. I felt hurt by my parents but at the same time I was defiant.

I had two jobs at the time in Cheyenne; working as a DJ at the Christian radio station, and working at the airport fueling planes. During that summer in Cheyenne I met other gay men, as well as attended an Assemblies of God church. One evening the church had a Christian singing group called, "Festival of Praise," which was associated with Thurlow Spur and the Jim and Tammy Faye Baker, PTL Club from the television show. They were looking for people to audition and go on tour with them, so I auditioned and I made it. A few months later I left my jobs and went on a three-month tour up and down the east coast with Festival of Praise.

While on tour I again ran into a couple of gay men who were also dealing with being gay and Christian. I used to pray and cry because I couldn't get God to change me into being straight. It was after this tour that it finally was sinking in that God was not going to take this away and that maybe this was the way God had made me.

My good friend David Virili was one of the guys on the tour that I confided in and it was good to have another Christian at the time going through the same struggle. After I got off the tour, my father got me a job for the summer with my uncle working on his supply boat servicing the oil rigs down in the Gulf of Mexico.

After that summer, I came back to Cheyenne and found an apartment, and got a job selling Kirby Vacuum cleaners. This job was lucrative at first, but eventually because the economy was so bad in 1982 I eventually had to try to find something different. I wasn't happy. With no money for college, and the job going nowhere, I decided to follow my fathers' advice and I made a decision to join the Air Force just as he had.

My father had served twenty years in the Air Force. One morning I called the Air Force recruiter and scheduled an appointment for the next day to meet him.

As I walked into the building I realized by the locked door that the Air Force recruiter was not in yet. I sat in the lobby of the recruiter's offices. All of the services had their offices right next to one another.

Now the reason I had made a decision to go into the Air Force was based on my knowledge or perception of the services up to that point. I didn't want to go into the Navy as I had my fill of living on a boat after working down in the Gulf with my uncle and I didn't want to live on a boat ever again. I really had no desire to join the Army, and the Marine Corps never even entered my mind. The Air Force though, I was very familiar with based on my father's experience and I had met some gay Air Force guys while living in Cheyenne. I also wanted to learn how to fly. All reasons why to join the Air Force.

As I sat there waiting for the Air Force recruiter to show up, a Marine Gunnery Sergeant walked out into the lobby and asked me who I was waiting for. After I explained to him that I was waiting on the Air Force recruiter he asked me why I wanted to go into the Air Force. After I explained that I wanted to fly planes he said that he could help me and wanted to know if I wanted to take a look at what the Marines had to offer. I told him, "okay," but I was still planning on joining the Air Force. I was ready to join the military that day, and it was going to be the Air Force.

As I went into the Marine Corps office I sat down, and the Gunnery Sergeant and another Marine told me how I could become a pilot, after getting a degree in the Marines. They sold me a pretty good story. An hour later I was signing paperwork to go into the Marines. Because the job selling Kirbys was not working out I wanted to go to boot camp as soon as possible so I signed up to go as a reservist in the Marines so that I could go to boot camp sooner and also to come back and finish college.

As I sat there filling out the paperwork, I was going through and answering the questions, yes or no. I do remember the homosexual question on the forms, "Have you ever engaged in homosexual activity (sexual relations with another person of the same sex)?" I knew that if I was to get into the military I had to initial in the "no" block for that question. No second thought on that one. I was on the fence in my mind anyway as to my eventual sexual orientation and the way I viewed this is that it was nobody's business whom I had sex with.

After filling out the forms I shook hands with the recruiter and made an appointment for when I was going to ship out. As I walked out of the recruiting station I was on cloud nine. I really felt like I had made the right decision and I was about ready to embark on a new path in my life!

My father was quite surprised by my decision to enlist in the Marines but he really didn't say much. Nothing came up in my conversation with my parents about being gay and going into the Marines. My parents and I had not had a discussion about me being gay for more than a year now. I was in a Don't Ask, Don't Tell relationship with them.

As I waited to be shipped out in November of 1982 to boot camp in San Diego, I saw the movies "Making Love" and "First Blood" at the main theater at the only mall in Cheyenne. My first gay movie and a motivating war movie. Both gave me a lot to think about as I waited to go to boot camp.

Up until now I had obeyed and followed my parents, teachers and my church's rules, and yet something was still missing as I tried to find acceptance in my life and discover who I was. Maybe I would find what I was searching for in the Marines.

CHAPTER 5
BOOT CAMP

0900 hours 29 November 1982 Cheyenne, Wyoming

It was early in the morning as I headed down to the recruiting office to leave Cheyenne. I was supposed to meet up at the recruiting office with the recruiter and some other guys going into the military, to take a van down to Denver, Colorado to the Military Entrance Processing Station, (MEPS) so that we could go through processing before catching a flight to San Diego for boot camp. The drive from Cheyenne to Denver is about two hours.

The Marine Corps has two Recruit depots (boot camps) in the United States. Everyone that lives in the western part of the U.S. going into the Marines gets shipped to San Diego, California and everyone living in the eastern part of the U.S. goes to Parris Island, South Carolina.

According to my recruiter, I would be going down to Denver and staying in a hotel for the night with a bunch of other inductees going into the services and then process through MEPS the next day and then leave for San Diego that evening.

Once we got down to Denver we checked into a hotel and I was assigned to a room with some other guys from Colorado who also were about ready to leave for boot camp. I got my room key from the desk and walked up to the second floor. As I got to the hotel room I found three other guys already there, drinking and playing quarters around a small table. After some introductions, I found out that a couple of the guys were going into the Army and one was going into the Navy.

Even though we were not supposed to be drinking the day before getting shipped out, I found myself joining them in the game
of quarters and getting smashed. After a couple of hours of playing
I was really drunk, as we all got ready to crash for the night.

The problem was that there were four of us and only two
queen-size beds. That meant that we would have to share the beds.
I was so tired that I quickly climbed into one of the beds and made
sure I was clearly way on the side of the bed, as I didn't want these
guys to think that I was gay. I fell fast asleep. Somewhere around
0400 hours I woke up, and to my surprise I was laying next to the
other guy and we were touching.

I got a sense that he was awake as well. So here I found myself
lying next to this guy and he is pretending to be asleep and touching me. My heart was pounding and I didn't know what to do.
As I laid there I heard him breathing like he was sleeping, and I
remember he turned in his sleep and put his arm around me. I
was trembling and I thought okay, two can play this game of "I am
asleep as well."

My mind was racing as I was trying to figure out what to do
next. So I turned over and I placed my arm around his body and
put my hand on his stomach. He didn't move away. This game went
on for a bit and at some point I realized that he had a hard-on. But
as he was about ready to turn over again, the alarm went off in the
room, waking everyone up.

I was frustrated and scared at the same time. I moved away
from him and nothing was ever said. We all got up, showered and
got dressed and got in the van for the ten minute ride down to
MEPS. The day was long as we had to go through final physicals
and sign tons of paperwork.

Finally around 1800 hours in the evening we got our plane
tickets and got in a bus headed for the airport. The flight to San
Diego went quickly and was filled with a lot of guys headed for
boot camp. As soon as we landed in San Diego it was late, around

2200 hours, and we all got onto a bus at the airport and headed to Marine Corps Recruit Depot which was right next to the airport.

As soon as we got onto the base the bus stopped in front of this building that looked like a barracks. The bus driver told us to hold on a minute and they would tell us where to go. As we sat there, a drill instructor came onto the bus and let loose on us. He started yelling for us to get off the bus and stand on the yellow foot prints painted on the pavement outside.

I, along with about thirty other guys, jumped up and started climbing over one another to get off the bus like it was on fire. I found a set of yellow footprints to stand on as I stood there in shock. I was thinking to myself what the hell had I gotten into. I had never really thought about how we would be treated in boot camp but now it was becoming fully clear rather fast that this was not going to be fun at all.

They marched us into this building where the first thing to happen was that we all got haircuts. The haircut took about one minute. Later on I would look at myself in the mirror and thought about how I looked like a shocked prisoner of war with that haircut. After that, we then were marched into another room where they had us put all our personal effects into bags and we were issued new gear.

Around 0300 hours, we finally got to our barracks, where I lay there that first night in the rack and started rubbing my head because of the loss of my hair and thought to myself what the heck had I gotten myself into?

The next morning came early as we were introduced to our new drill instructors and found out what battalion and platoon we would be in. I was assigned to First Battalion, Platoon 1114. We had four drill instructors; One Senior Drill instructor, Staff Sergeant Arndt and three others; Staff Sergeant Rattee, Staff Sergeant Medina and Staff Sergeant Lucero.

When we were introduced to them we were sitting in our

43

squad bay where we would spend the next three months of hell. The squad bay was a huge room with racks (beds) on either side and at one end of the huge room was the drill instructors' office and a clear area that they liked to call their quarter deck. We were sitting on the cement floor (quarter deck) cross legged in a formation when the drill instructors were introduced to us. They immediately started yelling at us and playing mental games with us, letting us know that they would be in charge for the next three months.

In boot camp, it was the drill instructors' mission to stress out the recruits mentally to see if we would break, and at the same time get us in shape. Marine Corps boot camp is longer and more rigorous and considered the toughest of all the services.

Most of the time the drill instructors exercise of choice for us was called "bends and thrusts." These were not new or hard for me as I used to do these quite a bit in wrestling in high school. What I found difficult in boot camp was the running because I was not used to that. On our first day with our new drill instructors we were in the front of the squad bay and we were doing exercises, when drill instructor Staff Sergeant Medina suddenly yelled "stop!" He then proceeded to say, "Who the fuck shit their drawers up here on my quarter deck?"

Standing there, at any other time in my life this would have been really funny, but right then I was scared, and I couldn't figure out what the heck was going on. That was until the biggest guy in our platoon, who looked like a big line backer, admitted to the drill instructor that he had shit his pants. As I look back on this later it was rather funny to see this big guy shit his drawers. But right then and there it was not funny in that stressful environment.

I always tell friends that if you want a good representation of Marine Corps Boot Camp you should watch the movie "Full Metal Jacket." Our drill instructors had a good skill of picking up on any weaknesses or traits in recruits that they could exploit, whether it was mental or physical. For example, there was one guy in our platoon who had a really high voice and they immediately jumped on that and called him a faggot throughout boot camp.

When it came to me, there were two things that they jumped on. First thing was they found out I was from Wyoming. So they loved to say "that there are only two things that come out of Wyoming; Steers and Queers and I don't see any horns on you."

Also I had a bad habit of smiling a lot. The drill instructors would come up to each of us and yell in our faces or ask us questions. Sometimes they were just inches from our faces. And I would usually start smiling when they would come up and stare in my face and ask me questions. Staff Sergeant Arndt could always get me to smile by doing that. I think it was because I thought he was cute and when he looked me in the face he would smirk and so that just got me to smirking as well, and in trouble.

Out of all the drill instructors, Staff Sergeant Lucero gave me the hardest time. Every time that I smiled he asked me if I wanted to fuck him. Now all of the recruits in our platoon were teased at one time or another for being a fag, it was just part of the many mental mind games that they played with us. However I was surprised at how much of the mental games in boot camp were about gay sex. There was no such thing as personal space in boot camp, and the drill instructors were always making homosexual references when they had us in positions whereby we were in close spaces.

"Assholes to belly buttons, like your fucking your buddy in front of you" was one of their favorite sayings when they wanted us to get close to each other in line. Because I knew that I was really hiding it in my life, I was particularly conscious of these gay reference mind games, especially when they directed these comments to me. I was also aware that how I reacted to this line of mental stress, might give my secret away. I tried as best as I could to mask this part of me.

The whole time I was in boot camp I rarely thought about sex or was sexually aroused because of the stress of the environment.

When the drill instructors would start yelling I would often get an upset stomach as this brought back memories of my father yelling at me and the consequences that came with it.

Days and weeks went by, and I continued to play by the rules and get ahead in the Platoon. Boot camp was a competitive environment. Every Platoon had certain jobs that were assigned to those who stood out; I was assigned as the Platoon Scribe. The top jobs were: Squad leaders, a Platoon Guide and a Platoon Scribe. The drill instructors said I had high test scores on initial entrance tests when it came to language and writing. My job as Platoon Scribe was to help the drill instructors with paperwork for the platoon. Unfortunately, this gave Staff Sergeant Lucero more time to focus on me. He was always looking at me in an odd way, like he knew something was up about me. He was the one that was the meanest and would always tease me about being gay.

Two of the things that the drill instructors used to play mind games with the recruits were; that the airport was close to the base and the other was in the evenings during mail call. When we used to do Physical Training, "PT" it was right along side of the fence by the runway. The drill instructors used to say that our escape was only over that fence and they encouraged it in a sadistic way. It was all a mind game to see if we would crack. It was not fun to look through the fence and see freedom on the other side.

The other thing that they loved to give recruits a hard time over was the mail that we received during the evenings when we had to shit, shower and shave before hitting the rack for the night. They used to make fun of recruits letters from their girlfriends and parents. I never cried in boot camp; however I did see other guys cry because of this ribbing. It usually was when the drill instructors were teasing them about their families. A lot of my fellow recruits I knew went through some type of depression at one time or another in boot camp from being homesick and missing family members and home. I however had the uniqueness that I didn't get homesick like a lot of the other recruits did because I really didn't have a close relationship with my parents at the time and I didn't miss Wyoming. So I never got depressed or homesick and it was a blessing that I didn't have that hanging over me. It meant though that I had nothing to go back to if I got kicked out, so it just made me that much more determined to succeed and make it through to graduation.

As we got closer to graduation the drill instructors were not as mean and in some cases treated us that last week like Marines instead of just recruits. When we would graduate most of us would graduate as privates but there was a chance that a small number of us would be meritoriously promoted to Private First Class based on our performance in boot camp. This was a standard practice. A week before we were to graduate I found out I was going to be one of those that would be promoted to Private First Class. Staff Sergeant Lucero however pointed out to me that week that even though the other drill instructors thought I should be promoted he didn't.

18 February 1983, was our last day of boot camp and our graduation. One of the things that really did hurt was that a lot of the guys' parents where coming to see the graduation. I had asked my parents to come and see me graduate but they said they couldn't. Based on what I had already been through with my parents this really didn't surprise me. After we graduated that day right after noon, everyone was really excited. It is tradition that you get congratulations from the drill instructors, parents and friends for becoming a new Marine. As I walked around to each of the drill instructors that day and got congratulations, one response was particularity jolting from only one of them. I walked over to Staff Sergeant Lucero and started to thank him. He gave me this disgusted look and refused to shake my hand and proceeded to tell me to get out of his face and that he hoped that he never saw

me again in the Marine Corps and that he knew I was gay. At this point I just turned around and walked away from him and took it in stride. I thought to myself, fuck him, because I knew I had played by their rules and I made the grade. The physical training, the mental games, the exhaustion and I had made it through the toughest boot camp when many others had not. I had worked hard, was meritoriously promoted and proved myself as a Marine. I earned the title of Marine and nobody could take that away from me. Years later while still in the Marines I looked back on this incident and I surmised that he probably had more to hide than me if he was so homophobic and could pick up on it. As the saying goes, those who yell loudest are usually closet cases, hiding their homosexuality themselves.

CHAPTER 6
ACCEPTANCE

2200 hours 18 February 1983 Jacksonville, North Carolina

After graduating from boot camp I didn't take any leave to go home but instead went directly to my Military Occupational School (MOS) for training in what my job would be in the Marine Corps. I was assigned as a 3043, which was a Supply Administration Clerk.

My MOS school was at Camp Johnson, North Carolina, which was a small base next to the huge Marine Corps Base, Camp Lejeune. I arrived in North Carolina on February 18, about a week before the classes were to begin. I was assigned to a squad bay and there was only one other Marine who, like me got there early. We quickly became friends and hung out together.

My time at Camp Johnson went quickly, as the school was only two months long. While I was there I heard of a gay bar out in town, but I didn't have transportation to get there and I really didn't want to get a taxi cab to go there as I was afraid that the driver would tell someone that I had wanted to go to a gay bar.

After MOS school I was then assigned back home to the reserve unit, MACS-23 Fourth MAW Buckley ANGB in Aurora, Colorado. I checked into my unit on 23 April 1983. This unit was only an hour and forty-five minutes away from Cheyenne, Wyoming.

Back in November, when I enlisted, I wanted to go to boot camp as soon as possible. So they initially signed me up as a reservist and told me that as soon as I went through boot camp and schooling and arrived at my reserve unit that I could then put in to go onto active duty. I soon found out that it was a more lengthy process than I had figured.

When I got back to Wyoming I talked to my parents and they agreed that I could stay in their empty RV on the farm as I worked and waited on my orders for active duty. In the mean time I got a job working at the Safeway grocery store in Cheyenne.

When I finally arrived at my reserve unit I ran into a guy in my platoon whom I suspected was gay. When I first met Corporal Eduardo, we hit it off right away. As I was talking to him we both looked at one another and smiled. There was this instant acknowledgement that we each knew something about the other but couldn't say anything until we were alone. As we got to talking, we played this game of cat and mouse, trying to figure out if each other was gay. This game I would find out was used a lot in the Marines to find out if someone was "family."

It is a game where you ask another guy a bunch of telling questions, like where he hangs out, what type of music he likes and so forth. How he answers those questions, along with his reactions and behavior, can give you clues as to whether he is gay or not.

After we both figured out each other's story, from there on out every drill weekend we hung out together after work. He took me to my first gay bar, which was a Country Western bar in Denver called "Charlie's." He also took me to one of the most infamous gay bathhouses at the time in the United States called "The Ballpark." It was famous for its design and the multiple floors, and had an indoor waterfall and cave. On one of my trips to The Ballpark, I met a guy named Jim Heiser, an Army guy who would later become one of my lifelong friends.

Eduardo also introduced me to the term "family," which is used by the gay community in the military to covertly describe someone who is gay. He also schooled me on watching out for the Naval Criminal Investigative Service, (NCIS), which I found out went to great lengths to investigate and discharge people who they thought were gay or lesbian.

During this time in the reserves as I was staying with my parents and working at the Safeway grocery store in Cheyenne, I was going to reserve weekends once a month down in Denver. One day when I came home from work at Safeway, my parents confronted me about some magazines that they had found in the RV where I was staying. While I was at work, my mother had gone through my stuff in the RV. To this day I don't know why she did it, but in her search through my stuff she found some gay porn magazines that I had hidden. When my parents confronted me about the magazines they told me I had to immediately move out.

If I was going to continue this "lifestyle," as my mother put it, then they would not let me stay on the farm. So with very little money, I had to find an apartment in Cheyenne. The problem was I was only making enough money to pay for an apartment, and nothing else. I didn't even have enough money for food. I went a couple of months with no money for gas and very little to eat. At times I was starving, and had no one to turn to.

To make money, I applied to do some Recruiting Assistance temporary duty at the local recruiting station until my orders came through to go on active duty.

I was promoted to Lance Corporal in October of 1983 and then started working full time as a Recruiter Aid in December. On 2 May 1984 I was meritoriously promoted to Corporal, due to the work I had been doing as a Recruiter's Aide.

A meritorious promotion in the Marine Corps to the next rank means that a person has gone above and beyond what is expected of them and they are promoted faster than the normal time and grade requires. The evaluations I received before I was transferred to my next duty station were 4.9, and 4.9. In the Marine Corps these are called Proficiency and Conduct Marks and Privates through Corporal get them, Sergeants and above get Fitness

Reports. I received excellent to outstanding marks all along and these were my highest yet. The highest you can get are 5.0 and 5.0. The Gunnery Sergeant that I worked for at the time, who gave me the 4.9 and 4.9 told me that he would have given me 5.0 and 5.0 but only Jesus Christ gets 5.0 in his book.

My orders came through in June and I was put on active duty and transferred to Marine Corps Air Station, Cherry Point, North Carolina. I really didn't have much to say to my parents before I left and was just happy get on active duty at this point and leave Wyoming and Colorado.

When I got to MCAS Cherry Point I was assigned to the Training/Education Directorate that supported the Harrier Aircraft Training Simulator and other various schools on the base. My job was to manage the property accounts. While stationed at Cherry Point, it took me about three months before I earned enough money to get a car. In the meantime I pretty much stuck to myself and life was just work, physical training and sleep. I didn't meet any other Marines or sailors during this time that I knew were gay. I eventually got enough money to buy an old used car. It was a 1970 Cadillac, a big red boat with big white seats. I loved that car and to this day wish I still had it. The weekend after buying the car I decided I would make the one-hour trip down to Jacksonville, North Carolina near Camp Lejeune to check out Friends Lounge, the gay bar that I had heard about.

That Friday night I showered and left to drive the hour-long trek down to Jacksonville. It was a full moon night with just a tinge of humidity. As soon as I got to Jacksonville, I had a hard time finding the club as it was dark and I was not at all familiar with the town. I finally found the building, which was on Lejeune Boulevard, the main road coming into Jacksonville and not far from the main gate of the Base.

It was a white cinder block building set back about fifty yards from the main road. There was no sign on the building. As I figured out what building it was I pulled off the road into the parking lot in front. There were three or four cars parked out front and then it looked like about fifty cars parked around behind the building. There was a guard in the parking lot between the front parking lot and back parking lot. As I was parking my car out front the guard came over and recommended that I park around back so that the NCIS couldn't see my car with its base sticker on the window or my license plate numbers.

What I found out later was that regularly, agents from NCIS watched the bar and wrote down license plate numbers from cars that were parked outside the bar. They would then track and watch people and put them on a list and many times notified their commands or people would sometimes later find themselves under investigation. Friends Lounge was on a list of businesses out in town that were considered off-limits for military personnel. The only reason it was on the list was because it was a gay establishment. NCIS clandestinely tracked people that went to the bar and was famous for ruining so many careers. It was crazy. I found out that this was the standard operating procedure for NCIS.

As soon as I parked my car around back I proceeded to the entrance at the back of the building. My heart was pounding as I walked to the entrance. This was only going to be the second gay bar that I was walking into and I didn't know what to expect. I was hoping to run into other Marines and sailors so that I would have someone to hang out with. As I walked through the back door of the building there was a short hallway leading to a window with a person inside that was checking ID's who would then buzz the door to let folks into the club. It seemed all very secretive and I found out later it was a procedure to try and keep NCIS out.

I showed my ID and paid the entrance fee and was buzzed into the bar. As I walked in, there was another short hallway with restrooms to the left. I then turned to my right and a doorway opened up to this huge bar. To the left were a couple of pool tables and to the right was a long bar, and at the other end of the building there was a huge dance floor. Friends Lounge was a drag queen show bar and had a large clientele.

I immediately went straight to the bar and bought a beer. As my eyes adjusted to the light in the bar I noticed a surprisingly large number of guys with military haircuts. That night I got up enough nerve to talk to a couple of people.

I ended up meeting some Marines that night from Camp Lejeune, but none from Cherry Point. The only person that night that I met from Cherry Point was a sailor named David VanDette, who was a Chaplain's Assistant at Cherry Point. We had a great conversation and he said he knew quite a few Marines at Cherry Point and said he could introduce me to some. I later found out the reason that David knew so many Marines and sailors at Cherry Point was that he hung out at the Snack Bar on base where there was a glory hole in the restroom. There were hundreds of Marines and sailors that he met this way. After a few weeks of going to Friends Lounge, I eventually started meeting more and more Marines and sailors that were stationed at Cherry Point. Some became good friends like Willie Torro, and Charlie Brown.

One Marine in particular that I was introduced to, Lance Corporal Len Regan, became my best friend while I was stationed at Cherry Point. He worked at LAAM Battalion on base at Cherry Point. We hit it off great right from the start and became best friends. Len and I started hanging out together and going to Friends Lounge regularly on the weekends. Over the next few months I met a large group of gay Marines and sailors from Camp Lejeune and a large group from Cherry Point as well. This large extended group from both of the bases contained several cliques that hung out together. This underground network in the military was extensive and I was always hearing of other groups that were not even a part of ours, but I never met them. One element of this underground network was that you had to be careful of who you let into the group as you never knew if someone was working in conjunction with NCIS. I later found out how important this was.

Weekends during the summer months consisted of going to Atlantic Beach during the day. One part of the beach was where the lesbians and gays hung out, and at night we would go to Friends Lounge to watch the drag shows.

One of the weekends at Friends Lounge, Len and I met a couple of hospital corpsman that worked at the Naval Hospital at Cherry Point; Bob Saringer and Bill Nay.

We all got along well and started hanging out together. Len and I would spend time at their apartment off-base at Cherry Point. Sometimes to get a break from Friends Lounge, Len and I would make the three-hour drive north to Norfolk, Virginia, where the Naval Base was, to go to the gay bars there. There was one gay bar in Norfolk called the "Late Show," which was a huge dance bar where you could always run into sailors. We would also sometimes drive two hours south to Fayetteville, North Carolina, which was where Fort Bragg is, to the gay bar there called, "OZ." You could always find dozens of Army guys at the bar. We used to hang out with a couple of Army guys, Kevin Lynch and Mark Ward whenever we went there. I also met an Army guy who was a Chinese Linguist stationed at Fort Bragg and we dated for a couple of months.

For the gay Marines and sailors at Cherry Point and Camp Lejeune, Friends Lounge was a godsend. It was a place to meet other military and to escape the pressures of being gay in the military and the fears that came with that. It was one big family. Friends Lounge was owned by Danny Leonard, aka "Brandy Alexander," a well-known drag queen in the south. Besides running the bar he was also a shoulder to lean on for many Marines and sailors just coming out and going to sometimes their first gay bar. He was also a fierce protector of many of us from the clandestine arm of the NCIS.

To say that every Marine who came to Friends Lounge was comfortable with their sexual orientation would be an incorrect assumption. What surprised me sometimes were the Marines who frequented the bar who would only pick up or go home with drag queens and they considered themselves "straight." I was really naïve at the time but learned quickly about the blurred lines in the Marine Corps between straight, bisexual, and gay, and how many Marines floated between the three. In a nutshell, Friends Lounge served as an oasis for those just coming out, questioning or who were very comfortable with their orientation.

I met some wonderful people who went to Friends Lounge that really influenced how I started thinking about being gay and in the Marine Corps. One night I was sitting at the bar and there was a Marine who was getting very drunk and was really depressed.

We started talking and I asked him what was wrong. He started to tell me a sad story. He was still mourning the loss of his lover who had been killed a year before in the 1984 bombing of the Marine Barracks in Beirut. The military, after the bombing, gave counseling to family members. Gay servicemembers, however, who had lovers killed couldn't participate to the extent that they needed or wanted to because the military couldn't know about their relationships.

This Marine that I was listening to wasn't able to share his grief with anyone at the time, and still continued to go through depression over his lover being killed. I often saw him getting drunk at the bar and having to be driven home by friends. Later I found out there were at least three other Marines and a couple of sailors that were in the same situation as he, where their partners were killed in the bombing, but no one could know. They had to suffer in silence. Listening to these heart-wrenching stories and meeting these people, I really started despising how the military treated gay and lesbian servicemembers.

It was in the first few months while stationed at Cherry Point, meeting all of these other gay military who were comfortable in their sexual orientation and in particular my close friendship with Len and his resolute acceptance of himself that I finally accepted myself for who I really was.

For the first time in my life I was truly happy. I gave up trying to pray away being gay. As soon as I did, a peace, joy, and assurance came into my life about who I was. I stopped being depressed about the issue as I accepted the fact that God made me this way. As soon as I accepted this fact, my self-esteem improved greatly.

It was at this point in my life that I decided to have a conversation with my parents again about being gay, hoping they would accept it and support me. I had seen other gay Marines and sailors who had supportive and loving parents who accepted their kids unconditionally and shared their lives with them. I was hoping that I could find that same relationship with my parents and get them to come around.

So one afternoon, while I was out at Bob and Bill's apartment off-base with Len, I called my parents to talk with them. The conversation started out with small talk, and then I told my mother that I had something to tell her. I told her that I was really happy. I explained to her that I had been praying all of these years growing up in church, for God to take away these feelings from me for being gay. I had cried over and over again and had been depressed, but now that I had joined the Marines and had met others like myself who were comfortable with who they were, I soon realized that God wasn't going to take this away and that he made me this way. I had felt a peace in my life and that I was not going to change.

Her response to me was short and condescending. "That's nice but it still means you will live in hell for eternity." My heart broke when I heard her say this. I realized that no amount of truth, logic or pleading would change her mind. And where my mother went my dad and brother would follow. My sister would later turn out to be the only one in the family to accept and support me.

The realization set in that there was no way that I would ever have the relationship with my parents that I had hoped for. My mother went on to say that they couldn't accept me for the way I was and that they would have to "love me from a distance," meaning that if I was going to continue down "this path" then they would not be able to be in my life until I changed. They were excommunicating me from their lives. All the while as she was telling me this, I thought back to how I had played by my parents' and church's rules while growing up and had been unhappy. It wasn't until I had gone into the Marine Corps and admitted that I was gay and started realizing that I didn't need to change, that I saw that some rules were made to be broken. I was accepting myself for who I was and the way God made me, and for once in my life I was truly happy. No more would I let the religious dogma, the guilt from my parents, continue to rule or control my life. Instinctively I knew at that point that if someone in your life is not furthering your positive growth as a human being and they are negatively affecting you, then they shouldn't be in your life. This was when I let go of my parents and realized I wasn't going to change their minds. My parents didn't love me unconditionally. Their personal Christian mantra which was repeated to me over and over again, "love the sinner, hate the sin" was conditional love and a hypocrisy.

The conversation ended rather abruptly as we both said, "okay" and that was that. My mother said "we will be praying for your soul that you change." After this conversation with my mother, it would be another four years before we would talk again, and at that point in my life, I then realized that Len, Bob, Bill and all of my fellow gay and lesbian friends in the military were my true family. The camaraderie and kinship and closeness in what we all shared in the military was true and right, and for the first time in my life I felt like I belonged and had people who cared about me. I stopped letting my parents rule my life and I realized who and what was really important in my life. I had finally found what I was looking for.

After seven months of being stationed at Cherry Point, Len and I had the opportunity to move off-base and live with Bob and Bill at their apartment. This was a really great opportunity for both of us to be able to live off-base and to give us some privacy. Around this time, Bob introduced me to a Naval doctor, John Conte, who was an Osteopath and worked at Cherry Point Naval Hospital. He was an amazing person who was very smart and comfortable in his sexual orientation. We went out on a couple of dates, but he eventually settled down with another Marine, Rick Martinez. John was a very good friend who gave me some good counsel on how to handle different situations and we continued to stay in touch long after I had left Cherry Point.

During my time stationed at Cherry Point, I started thinking about what I wanted to do in the Corps, and how far I wanted to go. I had aspirations of going on to be a Warrant Officer, but I had to finish college first. In April of 1985, I attended the Noncommissioned Officers Basic Course. I also attended the Officer and Noncommissioned Officer Nuclear, Biological and Chemical Defense Course.

In June of 1985 I got a Meritorious Mast from the Commanding Officer for my work at the Training/Education Directorate. I was the Non-Commissioned Officer in Charge (NCOIC) of the accounts in the government property section. He had put on the award the following:

"You have consistently set the example as a Marine NCO by your unselfish attitude, dedication, and performance as a leader of Marines. Your performance is in keeping with the highest tradition of the United States Marine Corps." Before I left MCAS Cherry Point, I was awarded a Certificate of Commendation from the Commanding General of MCAS Cherry Point, Brigadier General James Mead, for my work at the Training/Education Directorate. He wrote, "During this period Corporal Elzie displayed exceptional drive and technical expertise in implementing programs

59

to ensure the thorough accountability of the Training Director-ate's more than twenty-nine million dollar accountable assets. His tireless efforts and enthusiasm contributed significantly to the improved supply support extended to the twelve sub-accounts within his purview. Corporal Elzie's professional skill and loyal dedication to duty reflect great credit upon himself, this Command, and the Unites States Marine Corps."

In late September I got orders to report to a new command. I was getting stationed for the first time overseas. Company L, Marine Support Battalion, Naval Security Group Activity in Guantanamo Bay Cuba.

Before I left Cherry Point, we all found out that Bob was being investigated by the NCIS for being gay. This meant that we were all under suspicion since we all hung out together and we later were to find out that this was part of a much larger investigation involving several people at Cherry Point and Camp Lejeune. NCIS was being really evil in the way they were operating. One part of the investigation was that David Vandette had invited a "straight" sailor to one of the parties. He didn't know that this sailor was working with NCIS and was taking down people's names. This sailor turned in about fifteen names.

NCIS tried to turn people against one another as they were calling in gay Marines and sailors to interview and interrogate them by telling some of them that David had turned them in, which wasn't true, but some people believed it and later on David almost committed suicide over this.

The investigation continued long after I left Cherry Point. This whole investigation just highlighted for me how important it was to really be careful of whom you trusted and whom you let into your group that you ran around with. But it also made me despise more and more how the military and NCIS went after good people and ruined people's lives just because of the ban on gays in the military.

Even though Bob and several other people were under investigation and being questioned, Bob, Bill and Len decided to still throw me a huge going away barbeque at our off-base apartment. At least fifty people showed up, Marines and sailors from Cherry Point and Camp Lejeune and I got to say goodbye to a lot of my friends in the Marine Corps that day like Don Barefoot, Bill Bourassa, Brian Lightly, and of course, Len Regan. I had many good memories from my friendships with these Marines. Early in the morning of 29 September, 1985, I said goodbye to Len, Bob and Bill and left on a flight from Jacksonville, North Carolina to the Naval Base at Norfolk, Virginia to catch a flight to the Naval Base at Guantanamo Bay (GITMO), Cuba.

CHAPTER 7
GITMO

1400 hours 29 September 1985 Guantanamo Bay, Cuba

After a long flight from Norfolk I looked out the plane window to see the beautiful blue-green waters of the Caribbean as we started turning around the lower cape of Cuba to land at Guantanamo Bay. The plane captain came on the intercom to tell us that we would be landing soon. Within a few minutes, we had landed at the airport on the Naval Base. It was sunny compared to the clouds and rain that we had just left in Norfolk, Virginia. As soon as I stepped off the plane a blast of heat hit me and I began immediately sweating in the bright sun. I was definitely now in the Caribbean.

Being in Guantanamo Bay, Cuba was only the second time that I had been out of the country in my life. The weather, aromas, and environment were like nothing I had ever experienced living in the States. After getting off the plane I caught a ferry to go across the bay to the main side of the base.

The way GITMO is set up is that the airport is on the leeward side of the bay and the main base is on the windward side of the bay. As soon as I arrived on the windward side of the bay, I found out that all the Marines on the Naval Base lived up on a hill called Marine Hill. There were two Marine Corps commands on the base, Marine Barracks, which consisted of infantry and tanks to guard the fence line, and Company "L," which I was stationed with, supporting the U.S. Naval Security Group Activity on John Paul Jones Hill. As soon as I got to the windward side of the bay I checked in with my command. My job would be working in the Supply section and overseeing the budget.

I knew going to GITMO that I was basically going into an environment where there were no gay bars and I knew that I probably would be celibate for most of the time that I was there. Before I left Cherry Point I tried to find out if any of my friends knew anyone who was stationed at GITMO that was gay. The answer I got was no. It is common practice, that when you find out that you are going to another duty station, you tap into the underground network of lesbians and gays in the military to see if anyone knows someone at the base that you are going to so that they can introduce you to the people or groups that are there. But at GITMO I was walking into a foreign environment where I would have to rely on my instincts to survive.

After I had been at GITMO for a couple of months, I was at work one day when my Staff Sergeant that I worked for got a call from the NCIS saying that they wanted to interview me. The look on his face worried me. I was nervous as hell to why they wanted to talk to me, and I suspected it was because of the ongoing investigation at Cherry Point and Camp Lejeune.

So the next day this civilian guy showed up at work. He took me to one of the rooms in our building to interview me. It was just the two of us in the room, and with no one else around he started telling me why he was there. He said that he was here to ask me questions about Hospital Corpsman, Bob Saringer, my former roommate at Cherry Point. As soon as he mentioned Bob's name I was thinking to myself "Oh, Fuck." I was worried that he was going to say that someone had fingered me for being gay.

He however proceeded to tell me that they thought Bob was gay and that I could help him out a lot if I could tell him everything I knew about Bob and other people that were gay. He proceeded to try to befriend me and he said that I could help him out by giving him information on Bob or anyone else that was gay so that they could be discharged out of the military. He tried to make it sound as if he assumed that we both agreed that there should be no gays in the military. At this point I knew what was happening and his tactics. I knew NCIS had been watching all of us at Cherry Point. He suspected me of being gay as well, but the target was Bob and he was doing all he could to get me to spill anything I knew.

After he gave his spiel of what he wanted me to tell him, I sat there sweating as I proceeded to tell him that I thought what he and the rest of NCIS were doing was wrong. I then told him that I didn't have anything to say to him. End of conversation.

At that point he said, "okay" and left, while I sat there shaking with rage and nervousness, at the whole encounter. I was thinking, "what now?" but I never heard from him or anyone else from NCIS again after that. I had learned by that point in the Marine Corps, what NCIS used as tactics, and I knew that I didn't have to talk to them and that they had no jurisdiction over me.

In my time in the Marines up to that point I had seen them threaten and blackmail other Marines and sailors, and I knew what their limits were and there was no way they were going to get anything out of me. This, however, did cause me to be a lot more careful at GITMO, as I was sure they were watching me.

My time in Cuba was nice. One of the things people say when you get stationed overseas is that you do one of two things. Either you become a Bible Thumper, or you become a Gym Rat because there is nothing else to do on base when stationed overseas. I became a Gym Rat. It was in GITMO that I started lifting weights pretty seriously as well as played on our command soccer team.

On the weekends quite a few of us enjoyed snorkeling and barbeques on the coral beaches. I liked being stationed there so much that when it came time for me to go back to the States I extended my time in GITMO until my enlistment was up in May of 1987. I spent a total of twenty months at GITMO.

One of my favorite moments while at GITMO was when I got a chance to met Jacques Cousteau. He was doing a documentary on the waters and coral reefs of Cuba and was a guest on the base.

They took him up to the highest point on the base, to where I worked and I got a chance to meet and get my picture taken with him.

While stationed at GITMO I also went to my first annual Marine Corps Ball. Every year around the world the Marines celebrate the Marine Corps birthday on 10 November, commemorating the year the United States Marine Corps was founded in 1775.

It is a tradition that is steeped in ceremony and honor. We found out that General Alfred Gray, who was rumored to be in line to be the next Marine Commandant, would be at the ball.

It was one of the best Marine Corps balls of my career. My buddies and I got to meet and talk with General Gray. He was very popular with all of the enlisted because he was a former enlisted Marine, and he was also very personable. It was a very motivating point in my career.

There were two club on the base, one a sailors' club and one for the Marines up on Marine Hill. The Marine Club up on Marine Hill was usually pretty wild, especially when a Naval ship was in port because the sailors always wanted to go to the Marine Club instead of the Navy Club because it was better.

Going to the Marine Hill Club on the weekends was fun, but could be frustrating because it was a bunch of Marines just drinking and dancing, sometimes with each other, because of no women. I went home many nights frustrated and horny.

Because of the environment of constantly being on a base overseas, and the fear of being watched after my encounter with the NCIS agent, I never did meet anyone else that was gay on the base. I did eventually tell a couple of close straight friends of mine that were in my unit because I trusted them. They didn't have a problem with it and we all hung out together.

I did have one good friend who was a Sergeant on one of the line companies with Marine Barracks. When I saw him at the club on the weekends, we would drink and play this game of wrestling and playfully pinching each other's nipples constantly.

We were both gym rats, and I was trying to figure out if he was gay. I was sure he was based on his behavior and the look in his eyes that he gave me, but never really got the chance to find out because a couple of months later he disappeared. I found out later that one day while out on one of the Guard towers on the fence line he was shot at by the Cubans on the other side of the fence line, fell backwards off the tower and was medevaced to Norfolk, Virginia. I never saw or heard of what happened to him after that. I always regretted not acting on my instincts faster to get to know him better.

It was during this time that I was in GITMO that the infamous incident, played out in the movie "A Few Good Men," happened. Even though it didn't involve anyone from our command, which was separate from the Marine Barracks, I did hear details about the blanket party that happened to the young Marine and the Congressional Investigation that happened after that.

My career continued on an upward path while at GITMO. In October of 1986, I was selected as the Company Marine of the Quarter for the third quarter. The Commanding Officer Major Makuta wrote:

"Your selection has been based on your professional skill, devotion to duty, and qualities of leadership. Further, through your example and initiative, you have established high standards for your contemporaries and future candidates for this honor. I am extremely pleased to have a person of your caliber as a member of this command."

I also earned a Navy Achievement Medal before my next duty station. The reason I received this medal, which I tell people is why I have all my wrinkles on my face to show for it, was that I brought a lot of discipline to our Command Supply budget and automated it on a computer program.

When I first arrived at the command, they were doing all of the budgeting and accounting manually on paper. I spent many hours doing a total restructuring of the budget for efficient management. Because of my contributions, NSGA Guantanamo produced, in the words of the Commanding Officer, a "flawless FY-87 Budget submission and earned laudatory comments from Naval Security Group's head of budget operations" from the Pentagon.

Even though I was doing all of this, I was considering going back into the reserves at the end of my active duty to go back to school so I could come back on active duty as an officer. I was thinking that I would go back to school at Old Dominion University in Norfolk, Virginia.

So on May 18, 1987, at the end of my time in GITMO and the end of my active duty enlistment, I caught a flight back to Norfolk, Virginia and was briefly transferred to the Marine Barracks in Norfolk to be released from active duty into the reserves. I was going to make a go of it at school, but little did I know how hard it was going to be.

CHAPTER 8
DIRECTION

1000 hours 20 June 1987 Norfolk, Virginia

In the month that I had spent at Marine Barracks in Norfolk, Virginia after coming back from Cuba I was preparing to go back to college, finding a place to live, finding a job, and going into the Marine Corps reserves. I found a place to live in the neighborhood of Gent, which was considered at that time to be the gay ghetto of Norfolk, which is what I needed.

I had lived for almost two years not being around anybody who I knew to be gay, so I really wanted to get back into the community and find old friends, as well as make new ones. On July 6, I checked into my new reserve unit, MACS-24, Fourth Marine Aircraft Wing, in Virginia Beach.

It became pretty clear to me not long after getting off active duty that because of my lack of education it was hard to find a decent job that paid the bills and paid for school. I eventually found a job painting houses, but I was not very happy. The money didn't pay all of the bills and my search for money for college was going nowhere. I was hurting financially and started realizing that I had made a mistake leaving active duty and going into the reserves.

Also, in the civilian sector there wasn't the teamwork, camaraderie or the feeling of the "Band of Brothers" that I was used to in the Marine Corps. In August, 1987 I took a couple of weeks off from my day labor job painting houses to take a supply course out at Marine Corps Logistics Base, in Barstow, California with my reserve unit. Once I got back from this Temporary Active Duty

(TAD), I decided to put in for a transfer back to Active Duty to reenlist.

While I was in Norfolk, I started going out to the bars again, since I hadn't for the two years I was in GITMO. I went to the Oar House, Garage and the Boiler Room. The Oar House was a dance bar and there were a lot of Navy guys who went there. The Garage however, was more my style, as the crowd was more blue collar types and you could find Marines there.

I continued to lift weights at the main gym on base, and was surprised one afternoon when I walked into the locker room and changed out of my gear, grabbed my towel and decided to check out the steam room. I had not been there before and I really needed to relax after my workout.

I pulled the handle on the steam room door when all of a sudden I heard this loud shuffling inside the steam room. I walked in and there were about nine guys sitting in there and it was quiet. I closed the door and went to sit down. All of a sudden I noticed some hands moving between the guys and I knew right away that all of these guys in here had been fooling around before I walked in.

This to me was a new experience, as I hadn't been in this situation since I went to the gay baths in Denver. That day I found out that the gym on base was a regular place for the sailors and Marines to hook up and have fun. I stopped going after a couple of times as I was scared of NCIS coming in and arresting guys.

During the summer at the Oar House I met a Radioman in the Navy named Steven Cook. He and I spent quite a bit of time together in my time in Norfolk and took a weekend trip up to Annapolis, Maryland, where the Naval Academy is located, as his mother worked there.

On September 1, 1987 I was promoted to Sergeant, and in November I was able to start doing some active duty time with my reserve unit until my orders came through and I moved back on

69

the Amphibious Base in Virginia Beach.

My new roommate in the barracks was also a Marine who worked in the Armory on base, and he was crazy. He was from Tennessee and slept with his K-Bar knife under his pillow and used to sit in our barracks room wearing his confederate hat and talk about how the south would rise up again someday and win. Needless to say I never told him I was gay. Thank God I was dating a sailor, Mike Degutis, at the time, and didn't have to spend a lot of time in my room at the barracks.

I was starting to get depressed around this time, as it was taking the paperwork a long time to come through to get me back on active duty, and spending time with Mike really helped take away the sadness of not being back out in the fleet. Because Mike's roommate was away on temporary duty, I often stayed over in his barracks room.

In March of 1988 my orders came through to reenlist and I was set to ship out to Okinawa, Japan. The only thing that concerned me was since I had picked up Sergeant in the reserves, I would be reduced in rank, as was common practice by going back on active duty. So I would be going back in as a Corporal.

This just made me that more determined to pick Sergeant backup while I was in Okinawa. I had to say goodbye to Mike, which was difficult. Mike's companionship was special to me, however I was trying to learn to not get to close to other guys so that I wouldn't be hurt when I got transferred to other duty stations. Our lives were going in separate directions and starting over again was going to be hard.

Before I left Norfolk, I talked to the few gay sailors and Marines that I knew to see if they knew anybody in Okinawa where I was going. One Marine that I knew at the time had a friend who was not in Okinawa but was on his way to the Philippines at Subic Bay.

So one day this friend of mine introduced me to Tim Bergling over the phone and we decided that if we got the chance we would meet sometime in East Asia during the year. Before I left Norfolk for Okinawa I decided to reach out to my parents once more. The reason was that it had been four years and Mike, my boyfriend at the time, also had a difficult relationship with his father and finding acceptance and it was Mike who encouraged me to reach back out to them. It had been four years and I hoped that maybe they had changed in that time. So I gave them a call and made plans to stop out and see them on my way to Okinawa.

As soon as my orders came in, I decided to take some leave on the way to Japan. The last couple of weeks of March I set out on a bus across the United States and stopped in Wyoming to see my parents, as well as my brother who was attending the University of Wyoming.

I spent a couple of days with my parents and nothing was ever mentioned about me being gay. I basically had settled into a Don't Ask, Don't Tell relationship at the time with my parents. Nothing was really said, but my parents were amicable. After I left Wyoming I took a bus to San Diego and spent a couple of days there before taking the train to Los Angeles for the flight to Okinawa. While I was in San Diego, I checked out the bars that I had heard so much about as I wanted to run into some gay military guys on the west coast.

I visited Peacock Alley, The Boom Boom Room and the West Coast Production Company, where I ran into some Marines and sailors. One of the nights I was there I was propositioned by a guy at one of the bars into doing a porn movie but I turned it down. Later I found out there would be a huge scandal while I was in Okinawa in 1988—a bunch of Marines were caught in California doing gay porn.

I had a couple of nice days in the city before I jumped on a train headed for Los Angeles. On March 28, 1988 I got on a plane and headed for Okinawa, Japan for duty. The twelve-hour flight to Okinawa was long. When we landed at the airport in Okinawa they loaded us on buses to go to the different bases that we would be working at on the island. On Okinawa there are several Marine Bases and an Air Force Base; Camp Schwab was way up north and pretty isolated. Camp Hansen was next, going south, with Kinville, a rowdy town just right outside the base with many bars and Asian fast food places.

Kadena Air Force Base was also south near the center of the Island. Outside Kadena there were lots of popular bars, and it was a hot spot for a large part of the military population on Okinawa to party.

Camp Butler was near Kadena, and to the south was Marine Corps Air Station Futenma and then Camp Kinser further south almost to Naha, which was a big city on the south part of the island. As soon as I got on the bus I found out that I would be going north to Camp Hansen. I was getting stationed with Third Medical Battalion, Third FSSG.

After checking into Third Medical Battalion I met a hospital corpsman in the barracks that I thought might be gay. I asked him a few questions and after some conversation, my assumptions were confirmed. His name was Scott, and he gave me the low down on where and what to do in Okinawa. He said that there were a lot of gay military that hung out at a dance bar outside of Kadena called "Manhattans."

So that Saturday I took a bus south to Kadena to check it out. That night I walked into Manhattans, and after some walking around and getting a drink I kind of figured out who to talk to and who might be gay, as Manhattans was a mixed club.

That night I met Art, a Marine stationed at Camp Butler and who worked in public affairs. He and I became fast, close friends for the whole year that I was in Okinawa.

Weekends after that were either spent going south to party at Manhattans or staying up at Camp Hansen and going out to a club in Kinville called "GiGi's," a video bar that attracted gay Marines and sailors.

Over the course of the year in Okinawa I would meet other Marines, sailors and airmen who I would years later run into when I was stationed on the east coast after Desert Storm. People like Jennifer Doemland, Keri Ackerman, Will Horswood, Kristopher Knight, and Mark Evans.

My career continued to go well while I was in Okinawa. I got a Letter of Appreciation from the command and then was selected for NCO of the Quarter. Then my Sergeant Major put me in to compete for "Marine of the Year" for Third FSSG. I went before a board to compete and was selected. In January of 1989 I was promoted to Sergeant.

Right after I was promoted to Sergeant I put in for some leave and took a C-130 flight over to Clark Air Force Base in the Philippines. I was going to the Naval Base at Subic Bay to see my friend Tim Bergling, who I had been introduced to over the phone by another Marine when I was stationed in Norfolk, Virginia.

I spent a weekend in the Philippines, which was a nice change from Okinawa. One night, however, out on the town in Olongapo, which is a little seedy town right outside of the base, I had went looking for the local gay bar and ran into a male prostitute who told me that he could show me where it was.

We jumped into a jeepney, which looked like it belonged in a New Orleans Mardi Gras parade, and we took off down some dark streets. A couple of blocks later we stopped in front of some apartments. We got out and I followed him down an alley, when all of a sudden he pulled out a butcher knife and demanded that I take off my shoes and give him my wallet. Somehow he got between me and the end of the alley where the jeepney dropped us off at.

I quickly wrestled the butcher knife away from him and got out of there as fast as I could. Thank God I got out of the encounter with my wallet and body intact.

When I got back to Okinawa, a couple of weekends later, I was hanging out at the USO at Camp Butler. I was upstairs playing Centipede on the video games and a Marine who was also playing video games, was checking me out. We started playing the same game and started talking. His name was Bill.

The USO at Camp Butler at that time was known as a pick up spot. A lot of Marines would hang out there as there was a glory hole in the restroom. Bill and I spent some time together over the next month going out to eat at a few places off base and spent a couple of nights together at a local hotel. We had some good times together until he had to leave to go on the Team Spirit military exercise in March over to South Korea. We corresponded for a while, and he sent me pictures from South Korea, but eventually we lost contact.

I was really taken with Bill at the time and upset for a while after we lost contact. I had my heart broken over him. Later that month I got orders to go to Marine Security Guard (MSG) School in Quantico, Virginia. In the discussions of what to do next in my military career my Sergeant Major had recommended that I put in for Embassy Guard Duty.

Marines guard American Embassies overseas and one of the hardest schools in the Marines is the MSG School in Quantico. I almost put in for Drill Instructor School but thought twice about spending the next three years yelling at people and realized that was not for me.

Just before I left Okinawa all of my gay friends threw me a big party at GiGi's in Kinville. It was a great night and we all got trashed. Before I left Okinawa I got a Fitness Report which is the evaluation report for Sergeants and above. I was rated Outstanding and Excellent, which are the highest marks you can have, in all areas from leadership to initiative. The Captain that I worked for put in the remarks:

"Exhibited the abilities of a much more senior Marine in

his aggressive training of all Marines junior to him. Dedicated Marine. Aggressive never stop, can-do attitude and exceptional performance resulted in his being recommended for the Navy Achievement Medal."

On the last week of March 1989, I flew out of Okinawa, Japan on my way back to the United States. I was excited to be starting a special duty in the Marines and the challenges that came with that.

CHAPTER 9
COMING OF AGE

1000 hours 27 March 1989 San Diego, California

On the way to my next command, I decided to take a couple of days rest and relaxation in San Diego. I arrived on March 27. While in San Diego, I spent some time at Peacock Alley and met a sailor, Jim Dolbin. We spent a couple of days together, as he showed me the city. It was a nice change from Okinawa and we became lifelong friends. Later, he would send me music tapes from the United States, while I was stationed over in Europe. I also met some Marines who told me of a phenomenon in the Marine Corps on the west coast; on 10 November, when there are Marine Corps Balls celebrating the Marine Corps Birthday, there are ones that are all gay -- Enlisteds and Officers. I thought to myself that I was definitely going to go to one of those Marine Corps Balls, one day. On April 4, 1989 I checked into Marine Security Guard (MSG) Battalion School in Quantico, Virginia. While I was stationed in Quantico, going through MSG School I would take the Amtrak train on the weekends into DC to hang out.

My favorite bar was the DC Eagle, and still is to this day. I ran into a couple of Marines there who became close friends, John Eager and Ralph Curtis. John Eager and I spent a lot of time together and ran around a lot until I left for my first duty station on Embassy Duty in the Marine Corps. John was originally from Bronx, New York and he worked at Headquarters Marine Corps in Arlington, Virginia, which is just right across from the Pentagon.

One of the things that I really liked doing most in Okinawa

and Quantico at the time was formation running, calling cadence and running in the rain. I was good at calling cadence while running with the platoon. We were required to also go on long individual runs while at Quantico, and nothing was better for my spirit than running in the rain.

While at MSG School we were required to qualify with a .357 Magnum. I qualified as "Expert," and ended up being the "High Shooter" out of my class and was presented with a Marine Corps flag. I was also at the time a qualified "Expert" with the M-16 Rifle.

Near the end of school we found out what our first duty station would be, and mine ended up being the American Embassy in Helsinki, Finland.

One of the highlights of our school graduation on July 7, 1989 was that the Commandant of the Marine Corps, at the time, General Gray (whom I had met a couple of years earlier in GITMO), was the guest speaker.

I really looked up to General Gray, and was glad that I again got to meet him. It was during this time, stationed in school in Quantico and hanging out with Marines in D.C., that I heard the rumor going around in the Marine Corps that General Gray was gay. I didn't put much faith in it at the time.

On the July 14, I flew out of Dulles Airport, (one of the airports that serves D.C.) to Helsinki, Finland to meet my new detachment.

On Embassy Duty every Marine Detachment assigned to an embassy or consulate is usually small. The largest detachment at the time was in Paris, France. Our Marine Detachment in Helsinki was around eight to ten Marines, with a Detachment Commander who was a Staff Non-commissioned Officer (NCO) and an Assistant Detachment Commander who was an NCO.

While I was stationed in Helsinki, I had the pleasure of meeting President George H.W. Bush, and his wife Barbara. They were there for the Bush-Gorbachev Summit of September, 1990. During the time I was in Helsinki I obviously went out to some of the gay bars. One night I met a Finnish guy who was what one would consider a "Tom of Finland" type at one of the bars. He was tall, blond, good looking and a biker. His name was Kari. He would come over to the Marine House and pick me up on his motorcycle and we spent a lot of time together.

We started dating, and stayed together until I left Helsinki. I brought him to a couple of the parties that we had at the Marine House, and I told a couple of the Marines in confidence that I was gay. The fact is most everyone already knew I was gay, and didn't have a problem with it. Leaving Helsinki was hard because I had fallen in love with Kari and we had gotten quite close. But like my prior relationship with Michael Degutis, there always came a time in the military when you knew you had to move on. You learned to put up walls so that you didn't have to commit fully, so you didn't get hurt. If you're always moving around in the military and gay it really can be hard to have a committed life partner because you can't get married and it can be dangerous if people find out about your relationship.

In October 1990, I got orders to go to my second posting on Embassy Duty. It was the American Consulate in Alexandria, Egypt. The Marine Detachment in Alexandria was much smaller than Helsinki. There were only five to six Marines, a Detachment Commander and an Assistant Detachment Commander.

Once I had been stationed there for about five months I was promoted to Assistant Detachment Commander. My situation in Egypt was different, in that there were no gay bars in Egypt and I didn't feel as close to some of the Marines there. I kept my being gay a secret, and told only a couple of Marines.

A couple of us Marines would hang out at the Carlos Pub in the residential area of Roushdy in Alexandria Egypt. The pub was owned by Carlos, who was Portuguese. It was the main gathering place for expatriates in Alexandria. A lot of the British, French, Germans and Americans hung out there.

I was more interested in drinking with the Brits and playing darts than playing video games and watching American movies like some of the Marines did while in Egypt. I was more adventurous than the other Marines and during my time in Egypt I explored archaeological sites, climbed inside the pyramids, visited the Sphinx and did some exploring out in the western desert of Egypt on camping trips.

While I was in Egypt, Desert Storm was ramping up and the night the ground war started I was on duty guarding the Consulate and listening to the BBC as it was happening. It was a very surreal night.

While I was in Egypt, I knew I would be going back to the states soon after this duty station and I was getting more and more interested in getting involved and making a difference when I got back there. In October of 1991 the issue of gays in the military was getting a lot more press and coverage, since there were gays coming back from Desert Storm, and coming out of the closet.

There had been some letters to the editor in the newspaper "Stars and Stripes," which is a U.S. Armed Forces newspaper that is read by all of the military overseas. I decided to write a letter to the editor after I read a few negative letters to the editor about gays in the military. I pointed out in my letter that the military's own studies had shown that gays and lesbians were just as good as the average heterosexual, and that men and women of atypical sexual orientation can function appropriately in military units.

I went on to point out that the military had provided no evidence that homosexuals were incompatible with military service. I never said I was gay in the letter. I only pointed out that there currently were no problems with gays serving in the military. However because I had stuck up for gays and lesbians in the letter, it raised a few eyebrows.

In the military there was a general assumption that if you stick up for someone gay or support them serving you might also be

79

gay, lesbian or bisexual yourself.

I didn't care at this point, as I was becoming more aware of the world around me and what was important in my life. In my time in the military I had traveled all over the world and had seen many things. I was getting fed up with the way the military was treating gays and lesbians, whom I considered my family.

While I was in Egypt I was watching what was going on in the U.S., and the fight to get rid of the ban was heating up. I was becoming more aware of the battle that was coming for us to serve openly and I wanted to contribute. I made a decision that when I got back to the States I was going to get involved in helping get rid of the ban on gays in the military.

In November 1991, I reenlisted in the Marines for another four years. On my Fitness Reports during Embassy Duty I was rated as "outstanding" in all areas.

In my last Fitness Report upon leaving Egypt, the Detachment Commander wrote:

"Mature, versatile, confident. Performance is OUTSTAND-ING. Primary responsibilities include protection of: classified material; government property; and consulate personnel. As Assistant Detachment Commander, he has proven to be capable and extremely reliable. Sound decision maker. Utilizes all available resources to accomplish the mission. Precise thorough, and punctual. Welcomes new challenges. Leads from the front. Possesses excellent oral/written communication skills. Maintains a high degree of physical fitness. Demonstrates the ability to handle increased responsibility."

In December 1991 I received orders for Marine Corps Base Camp Lejeune, in North Carolina. On December 31, 1991 I caught a flight out of Cairo, Egypt back to the states. I was on my way back to the east coast, and a new life change that I sensed was coming.

CHAPTER 10
MAKING A DIFFERENCE

1200 hours 1 January 1992 Washington, DC

When I got back to the states January 1, I took the next couple of months just acclimating back into American society. I had been outside the U.S. for a good part of my career and I needed to spend some time buying a car and going out and meeting friends.

I was stationed with Headquarters Support Battalion, Marine Corps Base, Camp Lejeune, North Carolina. My job was working in the Morale, Welfare & Recreation (MWR) division, in the Property section.

Once I got a vehicle I decided to get out and explore. One of my first weekends back I went by Friends Lounge to find old friends and meet new people. I was surprised by how many folks I ran into that I knew from the past at other duty stations like Okinawa, Cherry Point, and many who had just came back from Desert Storm, and also new Marines I hadn't met before.

Over the course of the next year I reconnected or made new friends with Jennifer Doemland, Will Horswood, Keri Ackerman, Ralph Curtis, Bryan Clark, Tracey Gerald, Eric Lane, Paul Burnette, Bill Bourassa, Brian Damron, Angel Acevedo, Chuck Parker, just to name a few.

It really was still one big extended family, like it had been when I was here in the late '80's. One of the things I noticed becoming more common now was the number of people who were getting convenience marriages to protect themselves from the Naval Criminal Investigative Service (NCIS) and the military.

A convenience marriage is where a gay man marries a lesbian (usually both military) so that they stay "under the radar." A couple of my friends tried to talk me into doing this, but I decided against it because I was comfortable being gay and didn't want a convenience marriage messing up my life. For me, that would have gone too far to living a lie. However, I totally understood why some of my friends did it in order to protect themselves. I had, up to that point at times in the Marines, ridden the line between being in the closet and totally out, from putting a picture of my boyfriend on my desk at work, to not worrying anymore about going to the gay bars, to having a pink triangle sticker on the bumper of my car. I was getting to the point that I was not going to go out of my way to try to hide my life anymore to satisfy a discriminatory policy in the military.

What I found interesting as well were the stories that some Marines had coming back from Desert Storm. It seems while I was in Egypt there were a lot of Marines and sailors fooling around in Saudi Arabia and Kuwait in the dunes. As one of the Marines told me, "when someone thinks they may be about to die, certain things go out the window and wanting to get one last piece of ass or doing something they always wanted to do before getting killed, happens."

Jennifer Doemland also showed me a periodical underground newsletter that was circulated between a large group of gays and lesbians over in Saudi Arabia during Desert Storm. It was put together by Navy Corpsman Wil Dunn.

Danny Leonard still owned and ran Friends Lounge and was doing well. He was amazing. I also ran into an old friend, a drag queen named "Secret" who had been a regular at Friends Lounge for years. She was the best, and as anyone can attest to that went to Friends Lounge over the years, she could work the pole in the middle of the dance floor like no one else. Friends Lounge was still the gathering place and refuge for the gays and lesbians in the military. Eric Lane called Friends Lounge our own personal USO for gays and lesbians in the military. Danny always had a buffet of food for us during the holidays. I also started going up to D.C. on the weekends to venture out as I had some friends up there I knew while going through Marine Security Guard, (MSG) School in Quantico, Virginia.

Going out again and meeting other gay military folks, after being overseas on Embassy Duty for so long, was euphoric. It felt great being around so many of my extended "family" again. I was again getting used to the way the gay subculture was like on the east coast. The gay subculture in the military can be different between the two coasts of the U.S.

The west coast is more laid back, and the gay military generally find it easier to blend in, especially in the gay clubs located between San Diego and Los Angeles. On the east coast, however, it is harder to blend in to the general population going to the bars. NCIS seemed to watch the bars on the east coast closer.

On the east coast if you wanted to meet gay Army guys, you went to the bars in Fayetteville, North Carolina right outside Fort Bragg. If you wanted to meet gay Marines, you went to Friends Lounge in Jacksonville, North Carolina outside Camp Lejeune. If you wanted to meet gay sailors, then the bars in Norfolk, Virginia were the places to go. If you went out in D.C., you would find a large group from all of the services out in the clubs.

When up in D.C. I spent most of my time at the DC Eagle, which is a Levi/Leather/Bear bar and my favorite in D.C. In the process of going there I met some other Marines and one that was in "The Presidents Own" United States Marine Band. He became a good friend and we spent time together when I would visit D.C. One weekend night, a group of us that were in the military decided to go dancing at Tracks. Tracks was a huge, famous gay dance bar that was near the Navy Yard in D.C. and you could always find a lot of military there. I was there with my friend Mark Evans from

Okinawa, who was in the Air Force and was now stationed at Andrews, as well as a few other friends, Marines and sailors.

We were out on the dance floor and I made the remark, rather loudly, that "we had all of the services represented here except the Army." Low and behold, this cute guy with a military haircut dancing right next to us, turns around and says "I am in the Army." His name was Joe Granger. He was an Air Traffic Controller stationed at Ft. Belvoir and the Pentagon in D.C.

We hit it off right away and spent the night together in his apartment in Arlington, Virginia. We dated each other for the next two or three months and he came down to Camp Lejeune to visit me. We eventually broke up due to the distance, but we to this day remain close friends.

Keeping to my goals of getting involved and trying to make a difference, when I got back to the states, I reached out to the Gay, Lesbian, & Bisexual Veterans of America, (GLBVA). I also found out that the National Gay and Lesbian Task Force, (NGLTF) was having an event on June 24, in D.C., and some veterans were scheduled to speak.

In that same time period, some active duty members came out on national television to fight the ban on gays in the military. They were two Navy guys, Petty Officer First Class Keith Meinhold and Lieutenant JG Tracy Throne and Air Force Staff Sergeant Tom Paniccia. I thought all of these guys were amazing in what they were doing to make a difference. I really admired and respected how they were fighting the ban by coming out of the closet in the military.

In June I decided to take a couple of days off and go up to D.C. in the middle of the week to attend the NGLTF event. It was at the Hyatt Regency in Washington. When I got up there and parked my car, I walked into the hotel, and then found the room where the event was being held. As I was walking in, Lieutenant JG Tracy Throne was speaking at the podium. I just stood in the back of the room, listening.

I found myself standing next to an Army guy dressed in his uniform. I introduced myself and found out his name was Perry Watkins. He was very friendly, and quite a character as I was to later find out. Perry had been a Sergeant in the Army and was discharged in 1990 for being gay. He later had to take the Army to court because they had reenlisted him three times, knowing he was gay, and then later tried to discharge him.

Perry would become a close friend and confidant over the next year. Over the next few months I met quite a few people in the gay veterans' movement to get rid of the ban. People like Tanya Domi, who had been a Captain in the Army, Alan Stephens who had also been in the Army, and Gene Barfield who had been in the Navy. I would later call upon all of these close friends for advice and support.

At the time, presidential candidate Bill Clinton was promising he was going to get rid of the ban on gays in the military, and there was a lot of press coverage of the issue during the summer of 1992. I met some members of the news media through the gay veterans, and agreed to serve as a conduit.

I knew a lot of gay military, and how to help get active duty gay and lesbian servicemembers to talk to the press under the radar. I really wanted to help get the message out that there were a lot of gay military servicemembers and I wanted to make sure that their voice was heard in the fight against the ban.

I was really starting to become an activist behind the scenes. I was tired of the homophobia I heard every day in the Marines and the press, and I despised what NCIS continued to do by investigating, discharging and ruining people's lives.

In July of 1992, on a hot summer day in my barracks, I took notice of this handsome Marine who was on duty and decided to talk to him. My gaydar had gone off and I decided to find out if he was gay, or possibly bisexual. We started talking, and spent the next three hours together. We made plans to talk the next day and sure enough he came by my barracks room and we continued our conversation. After about another three hours, it became clear that we were both gay and we started hanging out together. His name was John Logan and he was a Corporal working at Marine Corps Base Disbursing at Camp Lejeune.

I really liked John's down to earth attitude and his maturity. He was from Salem, Massachusetts. We started dating and after a couple of months decided to move off base together. We moved into a trailer park in Hubert, North Carolina, which was just outside the side gate of Camp Lejeune.

In August 1992, in partnership with other gay veterans in North Carolina, I helped start a gay veterans group to become a chapter of the GLBVA. The name of the group that we started was called North Carolina Veterans Coalition. The mission of the group was to support and assist members of the Armed Forces affected by homophobia and to provide referrals and resources to individuals and organizations working toward the end of the ban on gays in the military.

In October 1992 there was a situation on the west coast where the San Francisco AIDS Foundation had an ad campaign called "Sex Is Good" for AIDS Awareness Month. One of the guys in the photo shoot just happened to have a Marine Corps tattoo and the Marine Corps got upset. They sent a threatening letter to the SF AIDS Foundation because of this.

The Marines letter to the Foundation at one point stated that,

"your use of our emblem could be viewed as tacit approval of homosexuality by the Marine Corps. As you are no doubt aware, neither the Marine Corps nor the Department of Defense permits homosexuals to serve in their uniformed ranks".

Pat Christen, the then executive director of the San Francisco AIDS foundation, refused to comment on this statement in the letter, only saying that "its insanity speaks for itself." When I saw this I was so happy that the San Francisco AIDS Foundation told the Marine Corps to go pound sand. After my experiences in the Marines over the past ten years I found this type of behavior by the Marine Corps to be very hypocritical and very much in keeping with how they try to use a heavy hand and control their image in the public eye.

In November 1992 Perry Watkins, (the veteran that I had met in the summer in D.C.) came to visit John and I in North Carolina, and stayed with us. He was kind enough to speak at an event we had for the North Carolina Veterans Coalition. Perry was the type of veteran that would tell it like it was, and he didn't mince words. He was a close friend and offered a lot of good advice to me on activism on the issue of the ban on gays in the military.

Around this time the connections that I had with the media, and the friendships I had with gay military servicemembers at Camp Lejeune, started paying off with articles and interviews appearing in the major news media. There were comments and quotes from gay Marines and sailors out of Camp Lejeune as I introduced gay military servicemembers to the news media confidentially.

In November 1992, Eric Schmitt of the *New York Times* wrote an article titled, "Gay Soldiers See Hope and Fear in Ban's End," and another Article in the *New York Times* in December 1992 titled, "Military's Gay Subculture: Off Limits But Flourishing." Then Patrick Pexton of the Navy Times in December wrote an article titled, "The Quiet Network of Gays Already In." Ben Stocking of the Raleigh News and Observer wrote an article titled, "Gay Troops Hoping Ban is Lifted so Lies Can End."

These articles, I know at the time, had to send the Pentagon up the wall. To have honest, hardworking, patriotic gay troops talking to the press, countering the Pentagon's statements and sharing their personal stories, did not look good for the Pentagon trying to portray that there were no gays in the military and they hurt unit morale.

One great quote by Wil Dunn, a Navy Corpsman out of Camp Lejeune was, "If everybody who is gay or lesbian in the military turned green you'd think it was Saint Patrick's Day." Even though only his first name was used in the article, Wil got called into his Commanding Officer's office the next week and was questioned about his participation in the article.

Many of the questions from the press were about showers and foxholes I was quoted in one of the articles myself as saying; "gays were in the foxholes in Desert Storm and they are in the showers now, and it's not a problem. And it won't become a problem even if the ban is lifted."

I also said in another article, "I want to prove that you can be gay in the Marine Corps and be successful." In the articles where they quoted me, I let them use my first name and that I was a thirty-year old Sergeant at Camp Lejeune. I would later find out that the Marine Corps used this information to find out who I was. It immediately put me under suspicion, and they started tracking me.

In December of 1992, I received orders to another command, within the same base (Marine Corps Base, Camp Lejeune). I was getting transferred to Marine Corps Base Logistics in the Base Food Service office helping order large equipment for the chow halls. It was around this time that I also made a major decision in my career in the Marines.

The Marine Corps and the Navy were trying to draw down the military from Desert Storm and were offering early outs, meaning they would buy out your contract if you met certain criteria. The program was called, Voluntary Separation Incentive / Special Separation Benefit, (VSI/SSB). If I put in for the program and was approved, I would get out of the Marine Corps in April 1993. Now in the year that I had been back in the States from Embassy Duty I had seen a lot and I was starting to get really involved in trying to make a difference in people's lives.

I realized that in order to do some of the things I wanted to do I would need to leave the Marine Corps, finish my college degree, and then possibly come back in the Marines, especially if Clinton got rid of the ban on gays in the military.

I put in for the program so that I could get the money and go back to school. The end of 1992 came fast and furious, as Clinton had just been elected and I was looking forward to getting out, going back to school, and John and I spending our lives together.

On January 7, 1993 I received a new Fitness Report from my command that I was leaving and I got "excellents" and "outstandings" in all areas. In the remarks of my Fitness Report they wrote:

"Demonstrated ability and desire to progress and will make excellent career Marine. Highly productive. Displayed confidence in own abilities that proved motivational to others. Great growth potential."

In January, 1993 the noise from the Pentagon had gone through the roof about President Clinton's stated desire to lift the ban on gays in the military. I was ecstatic that Clinton had been elected and I believed that he would keep his promise to strike down the ban on gays and lesbians in the military.

Near the end of the month of January, Clinton was meeting with chairman of Joint Chiefs of Staff, Colin Powell, as well as the other Service Chiefs, and they seemed to be winning the war in the public discourse of the issue of gays in the military.

So much was being said by the military in the press about how gays would be detrimental to the military. I was extremely frustrated because here I had served ten years in the Marines and, as I saw it, there was in no way that gay and lesbian servicemembers were detrimental to the military. We were already in the military, by the thousands. It was pure lies and I felt I needed to do all I could do to counteract these lies in the press that the military was spewing.

That last week of January things came to a head and Clinton

was about ready to make a decision. On Wednesday, January 27, I got home from work and I received a call from Danny Leonard of Friends Lounge. There was an ABC Evening News crew at the bar and they wanted to see if they could interview some gay military servicemembers anonymously. I quickly jumped into action and made several phone calls to some gay military servicemembers I knew and then made my way down to the bar that evening.

They wanted to interview us, make us unrecognizable, and adjust our voices so that we wouldn't be identifiable. All in all, I think they used three out of all the interviews they did that evening and it played on ABC World News Tonight with Peter Jennings.

After the interviews I was standing in the bar and talking to the newsman. He was telling me about the producer who was doing the segment, and it was the same producer that had helped Tracy Thorne and Keith Meinhold come out on ABC.

He then turns to me and asked, "Have you ever thought of coming out?" At that moment I was stunned. It was like a light bulb went off in my head and the answer that I had been looking for so long was just put in front of me.

I really hadn't thought about coming out at all, but at that moment it was as if I had been working toward this moment all of my life but hadn't realized it, and now here was the answer, the opportunity and the moment of truth.

Was I really ready to make a difference and step out of the shadows or was I just going to be a coward, back down, get out quietly and let the bigots in the Marine Corps continue to say in the press what they wanted to about gay Marines?

I turned to the newsman and I told him I would let him know tomorrow. I wanted to go home and talk this over with John, and I wanted to sleep on it, even though down deep in my heart I knew what I had to do. I drove out of the Friends Lounge parking lot that night, contemplating what the future would be like if I came out.

I got home and when I walked in the door I sat down on the

couch and told John what the newsman had proposed to me and I asked him what he thought of it. John had supported me in all that I was doing since we had met earlier in the summer, but now he was not at all supportive of me coming out. The reason was two-fold. First, it would ruin my career in the Marines and possibly his career as well. Second, he was also in the Marines and as my roommate people would suspect that he was gay and his life could be ruined.

That night we both went to bed and I had a difficult time sleeping. The next day I went to work and I thought long and hard about what the newsman had proposed to me. I thought if I got approved for the VSI / SSB program, which was very likely, I would be getting out in three months anyway and this would be my last opportunity to make a difference.

From what I had observed so far, the public and Congress didn't listen to veterans once they got out, but they did listen to active duty servicemembers. Also, no Marines had stood up to speak out against the ban on gays in the military like servicemembers from the other services had done. I thought I could make a difference and maybe change the Marine Corps.

This question had been laid before me. It seemed to me to be the next step in my evolution and growth as a person. Sitting in my office that Thursday morning I made the decision. I immediately called the reporter and told him I would do it. So he set up a time that we would meet the next day, Friday, in Jacksonville, off base, and do the interview to play on ABC World News Tonight.

After the phone call I felt like I had just made the biggest decision in my life and it was like I had turned a page and there was no going back. At the same time there was a knowing down deep in my soul that what I was doing was the right thing. That evening when I got home I told John, what I had done, and we had a fight about it. I felt that it was something that I needed to do it make a difference in the Marines.

Spiritually, down deep in my soul, I also knew I couldn't keep quiet any longer about who I was. I needed to stand up for once in my life and tell people that it is okay to be gay and that I was not going to be shamed any more by society for being gay. This was the way God made me. I was tired of lying and hiding who I really was and I felt like I would be a coward if I stayed in the closet and didn't stand up for what was right.

I had to make a stand for my fellow Marines, but also for the salvation of my being and my soul. John, on the other hand, was livid and at tears at what I was about to do. He would be put under the microscope.

He went to bed while I sat there on the couch thinking. I had played by the rules all along in my life. But now it was time to break a rule and try to change the United States Marine Corps for the better by coming out against a bad and discriminatory policy that hurt people.

CHAPTER 11
BLIND IDEALISM

I woke up Saturday morning, January 30, to a phone call from Eric Schmitt of the *New York Times*. I ran to the phone in the kitchen and gave him a quick interview. As soon as I hung up, I realized that I needed to get organized and figure out what to tell my superiors at work come Monday.

John woke up and walked into the kitchen as I got done with the interview. He was very upset with me and wouldn't even talk. I was now getting the silent treatment. I went out to get a cup of coffee and the morning newspaper. When I picked up the paper, I noticed a story about something that had happened the night before down in Wilmington, North Carolina, which is only an hour south of Camp Lejeune. Three Marines;—Lance Corporals Walter Watkins III, Patrick Cardone, and Colin Hunt—were charged with assaulting Crae Pridgen outside the gay bar "Mickey Ratz." Pridgen said his attackers yelled "Clinton must pay," referring to President Clinton's intention of lifting the ban on gays in the military.

This incident didn't surprise me at all, knowing all of the homophobic talk lately in the Marine Corps. As a matter of fact, a Staff Sergeant in my office had said not two weeks prior that "all gays should be shot."

The next day, Sunday, January 31, Schmitt's article, "Combat role of gays to be under review," appeared in the *New York Times*. He wrote that U.S. Secretary of Defense; Les Aspin, had directed the Pentagon to review whether to bar gays from combat and whether to give them separate barracks and showers. Tanya Domi, a military veteran and director of the Civil Rights Project at the National Gay and Lesbian Task Force (NGLTF) at the time said, "That's unacceptable." It was pointed out in the article that thousands of gays currently served in combat units. I was quoted in the article, too, saying that "I don't think they'll be able to do it practically." I was shocked that they would even think they could segregate gays in the military. Knowing how many gays were already in the military, the idea of segregation was ludicrous.

The rest of the weekend was non-eventful and I just talked with a few of my friends inside and outside the military as I prepared mentally for what was sure to come Monday morning.

On Monday, February 1, John had arranged for one of our mutual friends, a Navy Corpsman, to take him in to work. He was still angry at me and he didn't want to be seen with me, as he knew everyone would suspect that since he was my roommate he was gay. I realized over the course of the weekend that I would have to distance myself from all of my gay friends in the military to protect them. Just being seen with me could put their careers in jeopardy.

I felt so alone driving into work that morning. I picked up something to eat off base so that I didn't have to go to the chow hall. I then drove straight to my unit and walked into my office and went right to my desk. After being at work for about ten minutes, the Staff Sergeant who had said a couple of weeks prior in my office that "all gays should be shot," came by my desk, held out his hand, smiled, and said "you got a big pair of balls for what you did." He went on to apologize for his statement about gays and wished me luck.

A few minutes after my conversation with the Staff Sergeant, I was called into my Chief Warrant Officer's office. Now, you'll remember, I had called Chief Warrant Officer Johnson, my immediate supervisor, Friday night about an hour before the interview had played on ABC, on advice from my friend Tanya Domi. Chief

Warrant Officer Johnson that night was not very happy.

As soon as I walked into his office he proceeded to tell me sternly that he didn't think what I did was smart and I should have just kept quiet. He believed that I had done something wrong, and asked me why I had done it. I explained to him it was an issue of integrity and I felt I needed to take a personal stand.

I then had to go in to see Major Ribadeneira, who was Chief Warrant Officer Johnsons' boss. He asked me the same questions and discussed briefly the policy and what might happen. The Major said he respected my decision, and after our conversation he sent me to see the Company Commander, Major Rook, and the Company First Sergeant. They both asked why I came out and where the interview had taken place at. I told them the same thing I had told Chief Warrant Officer Johnson and Major Ribadeneira; it was an integrity issue and I felt I needed to take a personal stand.

Major Rook asked if I were a part of any group and I said it wouldn't be proper to answer that without first talking to a lawyer. I was already getting the feeling that they were all fishing for information that was not exactly relevant, and I wanted to make sure that I protected the identity of other gay military servicemembers. I was not stupid. I knew that as soon as my interview appeared on ABC, Friday night, the Naval Criminal Investigative Service, (NCIS) would be investigating me, looking into who I knew to find other gay military servicemembers.

The Major and First Sergeant both claimed they were worried about my safety. I wasn't worried about my safety at all. I knew I could take care of myself in any scrape. They both asked where I lived and my address and if I had any roommates. That was it for the questions. I didn't tell them anything they didn't already know or couldn't find out from my unit. During the conversations there were some questions about the press. They wanted to know if I had contacted them or if they contacted me. Then they told me that I should go see the Marine Corps Base Public Affairs officer, Major

Farrar.

After lunch, I went over to the Marine Corps Base Public Affairs office to see Major Farrar. Upon walking into his office, his first statement was, "you've really created a media circus." Lieutenant Juergeson then walked into the room and they asked me the same questions the other officers had asked me. They then talked about some basics in respect to the press. Most importantly, they demanded, I was not to wear my uniform off base, that doing so would look like I might be representing the Marine Corps. They also mentioned that on base interviews had to go through public affairs. I had never done or planned on doing any on base interviews, as the press had always wanted to interview me off base on my own time. I also had never done any interviews up to now on Marine Corps time and I had planned on continuing to do these interviews on my own time and not involve my work.

At this point I was starting to get a lot of requests for interviews and I knew I could manage those outside of my work hours off base. Major Farrar also wanted me to let them know when I got requests from the press and keep them notified. I took that request with a grain of salt, because I knew they wanted to control the message and I wasn't going to let the Marine Corps speak for me. I didn't trust them and if I could keep them off balance, so much the better. That way I could keep the issue in the press out in the open, where I knew I had a better chance of not letting the Marine Corps screw me and shuffle me out the back door quietly with a dishonorable discharge, as I had seen them do to so many other gays and lesbians in the military.

Major Farrar proceeded to tell me his views on gays in the military. He didn't think that gays should be in the military. Throughout the whole conversation I had the feeling that he was having a hard time accepting what was happening. I didn't trust him because he had already lied in a *New York Times* article just a month prior, in December 1992.

In that Times article, Major Farrar, the Marine Corps Base spokesman, had said of gay bars like Friends Lounge, "We don't sit and stake out these places and harass people." I knew this was untrue as I had friends that had been turned into their commands within that same month, just for going to Friends Lounge. To some in the Marine Corps there was no honor, integrity, or ethics when it came to digging out gays and lesbians.

After leaving the public affairs office Monday afternoon, I headed back to work and finished out the day. I was getting the cold shoulder by some people at work but I didn't let it affect me as I saw it as their problem, not mine. But I had a headache on my way driving home and I was hoping John would be in a better mood when I got back because I really needed a hug. That was not to be the case. John arrived home a few minutes after I did and he proceeded to tell me the treatment that he had gotten at work that day. There were Marines and civilians where he worked and they knew I was his roommate. So not only did he get the cold shoulder like I did by some people at work, but he had a few choice words with a couple of them. He was put on the spot and he told them he was not gay. Needless to say, he blamed me for all that happened to him. That night I had trouble sleeping.

A Few days passed. On Wednesday February 3, I was once again called into Chief Warrant Officer Johnsons' office. This time he was very upset. He had gotten a phone call from a reporter, Ben Stocking, at the Raleigh News and Observer. Stocking was doing a story and wanted to get Johnson's opinion on the issue. It was written all over his face that he couldn't deal with the press or the issue of gays in the military. He was very uncomfortable every time I talked to him.

On Friday, February 5, when I walked into my office I was told I had to go see the Battalion Commanding Officer, Colonel Kahl. He was the highest ranking person in my chain of command I would be seeing thus far since coming out. I went down to the

Battalion and walked into his office. He asked me to take a seat and then he sat down and, with a smirk on his face, he proceeded to tell me that I had caused "some waves." He said that they suspected I was gay a couple of months prior in November, 1992 when my first name was used in an article by the Associated Press. He said with a swagger that they had a whole laundry list of people that they were watching that they believed were gay. He also mentioned Friends Lounge and how they watched the place.

The Colonel then told me I had been approved for the Voluntary Separation Incentive / Special Separation Benefit (VSI/ SSB) program that I had requested in December. He told me that he recommended to Headquarters Marine Corps (HQMC) that since I was approved for the program that they keep my name on the list. He mentioned that I had "pissed off " some people at HQMC in Washington, D.C., and that some hardliners wanted me discharged. He said that I would still receive my VSI/SSB benefits as long as "I kept my mouth shut" and did not do any more interviews.

The problem was, at that point he didn't know that I had just done another interview for Ben Stocking with the Raleigh News and Observer and for Estes Thompson of the Associated Press. These articles had not come out yet and I wasn't about to tell him because I didn't want him to make some phone calls and get the stories pulled from running.

On Sunday, February 7, the articles were published. After working on this issue for almost a year, I had figured out it was important to get the truth out in the press. I was respectful of the Marine Corps, which I loved, but I wasn't going to be silent. I had no problems talking to the press as I wanted to tell them the truth about gays in the military, and try to break down some barriers and change people's minds. I had a message to get out and I was willing to talk to anyone who would listen. I wanted to make sure that people heard the truth. The Marine Corps on the other hand wanted to muzzle me and did not want it out that there were gay Marines and there were a lot of them, doing their jobs well.

Ben Stocking's article in the Raleigh News and Observer was titled, "As Debate rages over gays in the military, One Marine decides telling his secret is… A Matter of Dignity." Estes Thompson's AP piece was titled: "Gay Sergeant seeks his place in Marine Corps." Both of the articles centered on me and why I had come out. In the Raleigh News and Observer, Ben wrote about an incident that happened while he and I were having coffee in a restaurant in Jacksonville, North Carolina as he was interviewing me. A big Marine and a woman with him got up and walked out of the restaurant and gave me a dirty look as we were sitting there. I responded to Ben at the time, "screw him, I don't care what he thinks."

This type of reaction actually happened a few times when people recognized me. There were others though, after I came out who did come up to me, shook my hand, and told me to hang in there.

Stocking mentioned in the article my parents and how we had a strained relationship since they learned I was gay. I hadn't told them beforehand that I was coming out publicly. Personally, I didn't care what my parents thought as they had already made it clear to me that their love was conditional and my being gay was a condition they could not accept. My real family were my fellow gay and lesbian servicemembers. In the Associated Press article I explained what it was like to be gay and in the military. Thompson quoted me about what it was like before coming out. "It's been pretty stressful. You've got to be looking over your shoulder, having to watch what you say. Sometimes you realize that no matter how well you do your job, to the military you're not good enough." I also said that "I want to be able to serve my country and be judged on the way I do my job, not on my sexuality or my sexual preference. I don't take my sexuality to work. At work, I'm a sergeant. I conduct myself in a professional manner.

He then wrote about how opponents of gays in the military

99

point to close living quarters. I said: "I wouldn't go grab a guy in the shower. It's not professional as adults. We all live by rules of conduct. They say what about the foxholes and the showers? You tell them you're already showering with gays and you didn't know it and they haven't grabbed you. There are so many service people in now who are gay and people know it and it's not a big deal." That was the just of the articles. Over the weekend I read every article closely. I wanted to make sure that I was quoted right, and that the message that I was trying to get out about gays and lesbians in the military got out there right. The next week I went about my job normally at work. I was still getting the cold shoulder from some people but others were starting to loosen up and talk to me again. John was having his own issues at work, too. A couple of weeks later John got unexpected orders to be transferred to the Rifle Range. The Battalion and his office where he worked sent the orders down. He felt they did it as punishment because they knew he was my roommate and they wanted him out of the unit.

A week later, Wednesday, February 10, I was called in to see Battalion Commander Colonel Kahl again. It had been three working days since I had last met with him. As I reported to his office I noticed that my Company Commander, Major Rook was also in the Colonel's office. Colonel Kahl had in front of him a copy of the Associated Press article that had run that weekend. He asked me to have a seat and then proceeded to talk about the article and how I had not kept quiet. Because I had continued to make public remarks about being gay I would not receive my VSI/ SSB. He informed me that he had received a call from HQMC and that I had angered some people at HQMC and that my name was pulled off the list and another Marine would be put in my place. He said I had one of two choices; either take a voluntary discharge and get out quietly or take an involuntary discharge and go through discharge proceedings. He highly suggested that I get out quietly and not embarrass the Marine Corps anymore. His premise was that being gay was shameful and by talking about gay Marines in the Marines I was disgracing the Marine Corps.

The problem was Colonel Kahl didn't know me well enough to know that taking that approach would not work. It should have been clear to him by now that by me coming out on national television I didn't think that being gay was shameful or a disgrace to the Marine Corps. By this point in my life I had grown up and gained my self esteem and self worth and no more could anybody make me feel ashamed for being gay. I was not going to let the guilt about being gay that was put on me all my life affect me anymore. What surprised me even more was that they were pulling the retirement program VSI/SSB out from under me that I had been approved for and they were just going to kick me out the door. After spending ten long, hard, faithful years in the Marine Corps, this was totally unacceptable to me. I loved the Marine Corps but getting out quietly with no retirement would have ruined my life.

I sat there in front of the Colonel and let the two options that he had presented me, and what they were trying to do, sink in. I was momentarily overwhelmed with hurt and shock which then immediately turned into determination and resolve. I looked up at him and said "that's screwed up sir," and said it would be wrong for me to get out quietly and not get my retirement VSI/SSB program that I had been approved for. I said I was going to fight it. I was going to take the involuntary discharge option and go through discharge proceedings.

At that point he looked a bit surprised and then called into his office, Battalion Sergeant Major Jordan and Warrant Officer Templeman, who was the legal officer for the battalion. He told them to do the necessary paperwork and to send me over to Marine Corps Base Legal to talk to a military lawyer. At this point it was clear my idealism had gotten me into this. The question was, would it carry me through the coming battle of wills?

CHAPTER 12
THE STRUGGLE STARTS

1130 hours 10 February 1993 Camp Lejeune, North Carolina

That morning after I was told I was going to be discharged, I proceeded over to Marine Corps Base Legal and talked to Captain Lacon, who was a Senior Defense Counsel. He interviewed me, took down all my information, and said that he would check with Headquarters Marine Corps (HQMC) about my Voluntary Separation Incentive / Special Separation Benefit (VSI/SSB) program. Later that day I received a letter from my Company Commander, Major Rook, dated February 10. It was a "Notification of Separation Proceedings," along with a list of my rights. It said, "You are hereby notified that I intend to recommend to the Commanding General, Marine Corps Base, Camp Lejeune, North Carolina that you be discharged from the U.S. Marine Corps per paragraph 6207 by the reason of your admittance to being a homosexual." The letter went on to say that he was going to recommend that I receive an honorable discharge and that I had the right to request a hearing before an Administrative Discharge Board. The letter said that I had to respond on whether I wanted a hearing by February 16.

I went back to work and started making a mental list of the things I would have to do to fight this. That evening, I left work and went straight home and started making calls. I called several military veterans and prominent people that I knew who were working on the issue of gays in the military in Washington, DC and on the west coast. Tanya Domi, Alan Stephens, Bridget Wilson, and Mark Agrast were a few whom I called to get names of civilian attorneys who could represent me. Sitting in the kitchen that evening I spent three hours on the phone. It took me a couple of days to finally find a law firm which would interview me and see if they would take my case. Arnold & Porter, a law firm in Washington, D.C., initially took the case and I made arrangements to drive up to Washington the next week to see them.

The following day, Thursday, February 11, I went over to Marine Corps Base Legal to see Captain Lacon. As soon as I walked in the door he told me due to another case he was not going to be my military attorney but that First Lieutenant William Brown was available to take my case. He took me to Lieutenant Brown's office down the hall and introduced us. I spent the next hour talking to the Lieutenant as he gathered information about my case. Now, Captain Lacon and Lieutenant Brown both found out from HQMC that I had indeed been pulled out of the VSI/ SSB program. The first order of business for the Lieutenant and me was to respond to Major Rook's letter asking whether I wanted a discharge hearing. The problem was that because of the upcoming holiday weekend, we only had two working days to respond. So Lieutenant Brown put in a ten working day extension to respond to the "Notification of Separation Proceedings" letter and cited the need to confer with both military and civilian counsel. The next day our extension letter was approved.

In my day-to-day interaction with higher-ups at my command, because the Marine Corps was trying to discharge me, I didn't trust anyone. And as a general rule, even though I was treated with respect there was an attitude from most people that I had done something wrong, which was not the way I saw it. I had done nothing wrong by saying I was gay. I just wanted to continue my job and be treated like every other Marine. I wasn't looking for anything special. In the meeting with First Lieutenant Brown, who would be my military defense counsel, I had to feel comfortable that he was really on my side and would really do what he could to help me. He was up front with the way he felt about my situation. He told me he thought what the Marine Corps was doing to me was wrong, and that they should have just given me my VSI/SSB program and be done with it. He knew that I had an exemplary record in the Marines and he said he would do his best in representing me.

However, I was also aware, because of the controversial nature of this issue in the Marine Corps, and the backlash that had taken place already, that there may be pressure from higher ups in the Marine Corps on Marine Corps Base Legal, on Lieutenant Brown and others who dealt with me, with how much help I got and how the case was being handled. I didn't fully trust Lieutenant Brown until a week later when an incident occurred as I was trying to gather witnesses for my discharge hearing.

The next week, Lieutenant Brown and I were working on a list of people who could be witnesses to my character and my outstanding service in the Marines. One of the people I put on the list was a first cousin who was stationed on the same base I was. Captain Daniel Elzie was with 8th Engineer Support Battalion at Camp Lejeune. Lieutenant Brown was having me contact my witnesses, so I gave my cousin a call to talk to him and ask him to be a witness for me in my discharge hearing.

I gave him a call and we started out with some small talk. He then brought up my coming out and said I should have just kept quiet. I told him what had happened to me up to that point and that they were going to put me through a discharge hearing and I was calling friends and family to gather witnesses for my defense. I asked him if he would be a witness for me. He immediately said "no." He would not do it, because he didn't believe that gays should be in the military. At that point I was somewhat taken back and felt wounded. Here was my own flesh and blood, my own cousin, and he didn't want to have anything to do with me. I took a deep breath and said, "okay." That was pretty much the end of the call. He said "good luck" and I stoically said "yup." We have never talked again.

The next day when I went into Marine Corps Base Legal to see Lieutenant Brown I told him what had happened with my cousin. He just shook his head, saying he couldn't believe it. He said it showed the man had no integrity or honor as a Marine. At that moment, I had total trust in and the most upmost respect for Lieutenant Brown. He was the only Marine who up to this point stood up for me and was there for me. He espoused the Marine Corps "Band of Brothers Creed," which one of the tenets is that a Marine should not fail to come to his fellow Marine's aid in time of need. Like we always said in the Marines, "Take care of your fellow Marine."

I am sure my cousin, being my relative in the Marines, caught flak from other Marines about being my cousin. However, it sure didn't hurt him professionally. Within the next couple of years he would become the aide-de-camp to the Assistant Commandant of the Marine Corps.

On Wednesday, February 17, I put in the paperwork to take a day of leave so that I could go to the appointment with an attorney from Arnold & Porter in D.C. on Friday. However, Chief Warrant Officer Johnson, Major Rook and Colonel Kahl all denied my leave for Friday. It was crazy, as I had earned enough vacation days. They said going to see a civilian lawyer was an insufficient reason to go on leave. I was shocked. It was obvious they were trying to make things harder for me and were not willing to even let me go on leave for one day to see a civilian lawyer.

Lieutenant Brown couldn't believe his eyes when he saw the denial on my leave request. So I called in a favor from a friend, Mark Agrast who was a Senior Legislative Aide to Congressman Gerry Studs. Within the hour, my leave was approved. All of a sudden all of the officers in my chain of command seemed cooperative and willing to grant me leave. The next day, Thursday, February 18, as I was getting ready to go on leave, Colonel Kahl called Lieutenant Brown and me to his office. Battalion Sergeant Major Jordan also joined us.

As we sat down, Colonel Kahl handed us a piece of paper titled "Memo For The Record." It stated that the Marine Corps, after careful review of the case, including potential impact of the President's Executive Order supposedly coming in July, had decided to release me from active duty and put me into the standby reserves instead, pending a final Presidential Executive Order regarding my eligibility for continued military service. It went on to further say that my application for VSI/SSB would be held in abeyance until the President's action on the Department of Defense (DOD) policy was taken. I was advised that if the President's Executive decision rendered me ineligible for continued military service, I would be discharged and would not receive any VSI/SSB benefits, but if the President's Executive decision rendered me eligible for continued military service, my VSI/SSB benefits would be paid in full. "Conditional VSI/SSB."

I sat there in shock, as they were trying to pull a fast one on me. They wanted me to forgo a discharge hearing and just get out into the standby reserves without my VSI/SSB benefits and hope that the President was going to allow gays in the military. And if Clinton didn't, I would be screwed and not get the retirement I had worked so hard for.

There was no way I was going to trust President Clinton to get rid of the policy as he had already thrown gay and lesbian servicemembers under the bus by pulling back on his promise to get rid of the ban and was only going to do a six month review and then make a decision. Word in D.C. was that the ban might now go away. It was very clear the Marine Corps did not want to pay me my retirement benefits and didn't want me to have a discharge hearing, which would have created unwanted press. And it became clear now why they tried to deny my leave to meet with a civilian lawyer. As I sat there I looked over at First Lieutenant Brown and we both knew we needed to talk. So he told Colonel Kahl that we would need to confer and get back with them. A meeting was set up with them for a week later, on February 26. In the mean time I would meet with Lieutenant Brown and discuss this and I would be going to D.C. to meet with my attorneys.

I was so glad that evening to be getting out of Jacksonville, North Carolina and driving to Washington, D.C., six hours away, to find an attorney and see my friends in D.C. I needed a break.

The next day, after an overnight drive to D.C., I met with an attorney from Arnold & Porter, and was informed they couldn't take my case because other attorneys at the firm had agreed to assist the Clinton Administration in its review of the military policy.

However, the law firm of Covington & Burling had expressed an interest. I went over to Covington & Burling and to meet them, and found three amazing attorneys; Lanny Breuer, Christopher Sipes, and Allan Moore. They listened to my whole story and decided to take me on as a client pro bono. That was one of the best days of my life, as I saw things were starting to come together to fight this discharge.

That weekend I stayed in town with my good friend Joe Granger and saw a few of my friends out at the DC Eagle, a well-known gay bar. Being up in D.C. with my military friends who didn't have to hide from me and relaxing at the Eagle was a welcome respite to all that I had gone through so far.

The next week was pretty quiet on the legal front as Lieutenant Brown was working with my lawyers from Covington & Burling. Work was quiet and going as well as could be expected. I was recognized everywhere I went on base and I was getting straight stares and cold shoulders from most people. The one thing that I was good at was that I could walk into an office or a warehouse anywhere on base and as soon as I looked at the people I knew right away who had a problem with me and who didn't. It was intuitive based on their reactions, the looks I got, and an overall general feeling.

The reaction I got from specific Marines that I had to deal with varied. Usually Marines under my rank didn't change their behavior and were respectful. However, Marines my rank, Sergeant and up varied more. There were a couple of fellow Sergeants who were downright rude and tried to be intimidating, which didn't work on me. I just gave them an intimidating attitude back. I was not ashamed of being gay and I was a professional Marine and my attitude to them was "deal with it."

On the home front, John and I were not seeing a lot of each other now, as he was working at the Rifle Range which was a few miles out, at the edge of the base. He had finally come to grips with the whole situation and was there when I needed an ear, but things were tense between us still. At that early stage, he blamed me for everything he was going through and because I had chosen to come out over his wishes. That defining moment affected our relationship more than I could ever have anticipated.

A few weeks later, the last week in February, MTV came to Camp Lejeune to do interviews. I got a call from a producer at MTV about being interviewed and they also wanted to interview other gay military servicemembers. When they showed up in Jacksonville, they did the interviews of the gay military servicemembers at Friends Lounge. They interviewed a couple of military servicemembers, shadowing their faces on the screen. Chuck Parker was one of the Marines who were interviewed. They also interviewed the Marine Corps Base Public Affairs Officer, Major Farrar, who did exactly what he did in the *New York Times'* article; he lied on MTV, saying that there were "no witchhunts" for gays in the Marine Corps. Nothing could have been further from the truth.

On Friday, February 26, the scheduled meeting with Lieutenant Brown, Major Rook, Warrant Officer Templeman, and Major Breckenridge took place at the Battalion. Colonel Kahl was not at the meeting. Later, Major Breckenridge would become the recorder (prosecutor) at my Administrative Discharge Board. Major Breckenridge presented me with a paper for an entry into my Service Record that I was being offered "conditional VSI/ SSB." I had already conferred with Lieutenant Brown that I would not accept this and so I signed the paper saying that I would not accept "conditional VSI/SSB." It would have been suicide for me to sign that and quickly be discharged with no retirement benefits. I would have been depending on Clinton to get rid of the ban on gays, which was not looking good at that time.

After the meeting, the next few weeks were all about me continuing to do my job at the Base Food Service Office, and Lieutenant Brown working with my trio of lawyers, Lanny, Christopher, and Allan, preparing for my Administrative Discharge Board Hearing.

In late February an attorney, Martin Wright with Collier, Shannon, Rill, & Scott in D.C. heard my interview on National Public Radio, (NPR) and being a fellow Wyomingite, wrote a letter to our Senator, Alan K. Simpson, asking him to help me in my case. He pointed out that we all hailed from the "Equality State," Wyoming, which was the first state to grant women the right to vote, and the first state to elect a woman governor. With this letter, thanks to Martin, I was able to meet Senator Simpson in early March. It was a good meeting and the Senator seemed to have an open mind and sense of fairness about him on this issue. At the end of the meeting he said he would watch my case and my attorneys and I were to let him know if I ever needed any help.

In early March, a social organization called Onslow Area Society In Service (OASIS) in Jacksonville, North Carolina, whose mission was to increase its members' awareness of community issues through group discussions held a news conference in support of me.

On March 21, I flew to New York City with some other gay

military servicemembers who had also come out, because Richard Avedon was photographing us for a spread in The New Yorker magazine. The article would be coming out April 5. Photographed besides myself were, Army National Guard Captain Pam Mindt, Army National Guard Major Robert Harmon, Navy Corpsman Petty Officer Michael Vallejo, Navy Lieutenant Commander Fran Watson, Navy Lieutenant Zoe Dunning, and Navy Yeoman, Petty Officer Murphy Stovie. Meeting Richard Avedon was amazing and it was a high point in my life, and at the time a nice break from the stress in Camp Lejeune and my upcoming Administrative Discharge Board Hearing.

On March 24, there were a couple of Marine wives, one of them named Holly Koerber, at Camp Lejeune who organized a town hall meeting in Jacksonville, North Carolina. I was invited to be on a panel for a discussion. It was touted as an open public forum but close to 900 people showed up who were really angry about Clinton allowing gays in the military. At times, it seemed like a lynch mob in the auditorium with people shouting and waving bibles. It was quite rancorous and one-sided. There were a lot of anti-gay feelings.

The forum started with a thirty-minute debate between one of the Marine wives who organized the forum, and a director of programs for a community-based organization that counsels gays. Of course the two Marine wives who organized the event were anti-gay so it started out pretty raucous. After the debate, there was a panel of retired military personnel, and local writers. I was on the panel with Miriam Ben-Shalom who was with the Gay, Lesbian, and Bisexual Veterans of America (GLBVA). I agreed to participate in this forum because, as I had said at the time, "people need to get the emotionalism out of this and listen to facts. If we can influence even one person from tonight, it was important." I was hoping to change some minds at the event. The *New York Times*' Eric Schmitt, who had written a piece about me before, was there and published an article on the event the next day titled: "A Military Town Makes Its Anti-Gay Feelings Clear."

Even though this seemed like a pretty hopeless crowd, it didn't discourage me. I continued to do interviews and traveled to talk at events on my own time. I was fortunate to have a very good friend, Glenn Hargett, who owned a local radio station in Jacksonville, North Carolina. He was a great sounding board for things that came up that I had to deal with, and he gave me a lot of great advice on how to handle the media. He was always there for me. I consider him a mentor in my life and I owe him a lot.

On March 30, the day before my Administrative Discharge Board Hearing, my boyfriend John was called up to report to Marine Corps Base Legal and went through an interrogation by Major Breckenridge, who was presenting the Marine Corps case against me. He asked John if he was gay, to which John replied "no." Then the Major asked him if I went out to Friends Lounge, (the gay bar which was considered "off limits" to the Marines) who my friends were, and did John know any of them. John basically told him that our lives were separate and he didn't know anybody I hung out with. This of course was not true but it was clear that Major Breckenridge was trying to find out information to use against me and also to find other gays and lesbians that they could investigate and kick out of the military.

At the end of the conversation, the Major told John that he could go but that he might want to talk to him later. Before John walked out of the office, Major Breckenridge asked John if he thought that gays should be in the military. He wanted to know if John was sympathetic. If John would have said yes, then his orientation would be in question. If John said no, then the Major would have probably tried to use him against me. John answered him and said that he believed that anyone who passed boot camp should be allowed in.

Major Breckenridge didn't get what he wanted from John. My

case was only about status, according to the Marine Corps. In other words, I had said I was gay and that was enough in their eyes to try to discharge me. However they were not beyond also trying to find out if I had dated someone or had a special person in my life to try to make me look bad. Personally, I thought, what the heck was wrong with me having a boyfriend? If a straight Marine could have a girlfriend why couldn't I, as a gay Marine, have a boyfriend? This is America, right? Land of Equality, Life, Liberty, and the Pursuit of Happiness? My personal life at home was nobody's business, just like Major Breckenridge's personal life with his wife at home is nobody's business. But alas, the Marine Corps was operating under the assumption that being gay was wrong, and I didn't operate under the same assumption. The Marine Corps could not know that John was more than a roommate, or they would have just lumped that on to me as well. They also couldn't know about all my other gay military friends or their lives could be ruined as well. But it was entirely unethical for them to try to interrogate my friends just because they wanted to try to discredit me.

On Tuesday, March 30, the night before my Administrative Discharge Board hearing, I drove up to the University of North Carolina, (UNC) Chapel Hill at the invitation of Doug Ferguson to speak at the University's Lesbian and Gay Awareness Week, put on by UNC's Gay & Lesbian student group. It was really a great opportunity to talk to college students and let them know what it was like being a gay man in the military, and to answer their questions. I got a chance to explain the current military policies and how they affect gay and lesbian servicemembers. I told them "I don't take my homosexuality to work with me. I conduct myself professionally." I explained how investigations of suspected homosexuals were still under way in the military, and lists were being kept. I said that I stood by my decision to come out even though the Marines were putting me through the ringer. "I came out to make a positive difference, to try and dispel a lot of the stereotypical and the cultural myths." It was a nice break, getting out of Jacksonville for the night, as I had a lot on my mind about the next day's hearing.

Through these couple of months I had not been sleeping well and I was getting occasional headaches from the stress. But with some aspirin and coffee I was determined to press on. The way I saw it was, I had a mission to do and I was the only Marine who had stood up in the Marine Corps to fight this, and so there were a lot of people counting on me to do the right thing.

After getting back home late from Chapel Hill, I sat down on the couch and took a deep breath and just took a few moments to reflect on tomorrow's Administrative Discharge Board and all that had happened to me up to this point since coming out. This hearing would be one of the defining moments in my career, right after coming out on national television. I have to admit that my upbringing and the hardships that I went through in high school helped me get to this point of dealing with what the Marine Corps was trying to do to me. In a way, I had been trained for this very mission.

Over the last two months I had tried to use my access to the press to dispel myths about gays and lesbians in the Corps, and at the same time do my job and try save my career, or what was left of it. I was being quoted in the press as saying, "I just didn't think it was right to discharge people on the basis of their sexual orientation." In answering some of the reporters' questions leading up to the Administrative Discharge Board Hearing, I was quoted saying, "I hope to show that I have an outstanding record and should stay in the Marine Corps and to show that I'm just one of many people who is gay or lesbian and has an outstanding record in the military."

The thing was if they were going to take away the VSI/SSB program from me, then leave me in the military to finish out my three-year enlistment. I had an exemplary record so far and I hoped that they would look at that. I had always adhered to the fourteen Marine Corps Leadership traits; Integrity, Knowledge, Courage, Decisiveness, Dependability, Initiative, Tact, Judgment, Loyalty, Unselfishness, Endurance, Bearing, Enthusiasm and Justice. I just hoped that the Board members would do justice tomorrow and keep me in the Marines.

I got off the couch and went to the bedroom, set the alarm, took a couple of aspirin and fell into bed. I would need at least a good four hours of sleep to help me through tomorrow. Laying in bed, John reached over and put his arms around me and gave me a kiss, the first one in awhile, and told me to get a good night's sleep as I would need it tomorrow, and that he would be rooting for me. I started feeling good about tomorrow and I fell asleep.

CHAPTER 13
THE WORST DAY OF MY LIFE

0730 hours 31 March 1993 Camp Lejeune, North Carolina

Lanny, Christopher, Allan, Lieutenant Brown and I met at Marine Corps Base Legal and then made the short block walk down to the courthouse. The attorneys had warned me that they might try to go after me today in the hearing but I didn't let that idea really sink in until later, because I was trying to keep a positive, maybe somewhat unrealistic outlook on how things would go inside the court room. Whatever was going to happen today was really out of my hands. I would have to let my excellent record and career stand for itself. I hoped that the Marines would look at the facts and come through and do the right thing. I had been able to control so much up to now but this was out of my hands.

On the way over to the court house there were a lot of camera crews, but we just went straight into the courtroom. At 0800 hours my Discharge Proceedings started. In the court room were the Discharge Board Members who would decide my fate: Colonel Ronald Matthews, Lieutenant Colonel Charles Thornton, Major Glenn Spradling, First Sergeant Albert Goodman and Master Sergeant Jerry Holtry. Also in the courtroom was a Military Legal Advisor to the proceedings, Major Steven Hammond. Major Breckenridge was the "recorder" who would be presenting the Marine Corps case to discharge me. There was also an audience of about thirty people, including press.

The proceedings started out with all of the legal formalities afforded an Administrative Discharge Board, but it wasn't very

115

long into the proceedings that things got interesting. When it came time for my attorney Lanny Breuer to speak, he addressed the prior day's incident when Major Breckenridge had called John in and interrogated him.

Lanny Breuer: "Yesterday an incident of tremendous problem to us, of really great concern arose, and I would like the members of the board to know this, and I would like it to be put on the record. There have been no allegations ever of conduct, improper conduct by my client, and Major Breckenridge has notified us accordingly. However, yesterday I learned at the eve of this hearing that my client's roommate was summoned by Major Breckenridge and he was interrogated, at the eve of this hearing. He was asked whether my client had ever gone out on any kind of dates. He asked him if my client had ever gone to any prohibited establishments. Perhaps most upsetting, he asked my client's roommate, with no basis, what his sexual orientation was, a clear example and a clear attempt to intimidate him. He also asked the roommate of Sergeant Elzie what his opinion was about the ban on gays. Now we and I am not prepared here to fight this as a political issue. I am prepared to proceed exactly according to the Separation Manual, and I find it's highly inappropriate that intimidation is occurring, that Sergeant Elzie's roommate is summoned by a high-ranking officer and is asked about his own sexual orientation and is also asked to state to the Major what he own view is of the ban. It seems to me, members of the board, that this is exactly what the Marine Corps said it would not do, it would not engage in a witchhunt, it would not attempt to harass those who know Sergeant Elzie, or to harass Sergeant Elzie, but rather would proceed with this discharge hearing in full decorum and accordingly. And I would like the record to reflect on behalf of Sergeant Elzie, we object strenuously to the conduct that occurred yesterday, and I just want the record to be clear about that."

After Lanny made this statement, there were more legal for-

116

malities and asking the board questions. Then Major Breckenridge stepped forward to try to explain his behavior from the day prior.

Major Breckenridge: "I would state for the record, sir, regarding the interview of Sergeant Elzie's roommate, I also hold the billet at this installation as Chief Trial Counsel, Marine Corps Base. Upon information that Sergeant Elzie may have been engaged in improper conduct, I took the necessary steps to investigate that matter. Nothing came of it; there was no desire to raise it at this board."

The fact was, the Marine Corps was fishing. None of my conduct was improper, but there were many people, Marines and civilians off-base who wanted me gone from the Marines, who were feeding them "information." They all operated under the assumption that being gay was wrong, and as I've said, I operated under a different assumption, that it wasn't wrong to be gay.

Now it was time to start bringing up witnesses. Major Breckenridge called Chief Warrant Officer Johnson, my supervisor, to the stand. There was a discussion about my work since my coming out, between Major Breckenridge and Lanny Breuer, who had questioned Chief Warrant Officer Johnson. Johnson said that he would rate me as average to above average even though I had been rated as outstanding just three weeks prior to coming out.

Major Breckenridge was trying to prove that my work had been disrupted, but then Lanny got Johnson to admit that I had to go to legal many times by orders of my superiors since coming out. He also got Johnson to acknowledge that it was the fact that I had to go to legal several times that was disruptive to my work.

If the Marine Corps and those in my chain of command, like Chief Warrant Officer Johnson, had not been trying to kick me out, then I could have been at work more hours doing my job. Johnson believed that all of this was my own fault and not that of the Marines who were trying to fire me. He said I was professional, and admitted that I made an honest effort to do my job during

117

legal proceedings while the Marine Corps was trying to fire me.

This line of questioning by Major Breckenridge made it clear that contrary to my exemplary record and job performance, he was going to try to use my current supervisor, who thought I brought this on myself for saying I was gay, as a way to try to destroy my character and reputation. Of course, logic suggests that if I had been left alone by the Marine Corps, I could have been at work doing my job.

After some brief questions from the board members to Chief Warrant Officer Johnson, he was excused from the stand and there was a brief recess. I was starting to see that this day was going to be a lot harder than I thought. I felt that my own basic sense of what was ethically right, and justice and fairness, was only held by me and my attorneys in that room. As we walked back into the court room, I was already starting to get a headache and we were only two hours into the hearing!

When everyone was called back, Lanny presented quite a few documents to the court. He posed arguments about status versus conduct, stating, "This case is not right now about anything other than statements that Sergeant Elzie made when he said "I am gay." Lanny was pointing out that my case was about status not conduct and went on talking about the Marine Corps regulations.

Lanny Breuer: "Your purpose, your policy statement dealing with homosexuality, 6607.1, specifically says that the purpose of the policy of the Marine Corps dealing with homosexuality is "propensity to engage in homosexual conduct." It does not say that it's how someone thinks of himself, but propensity to engage in conduct."

Lanny talked a bit about some of the experts' conclusions in the documents that he was submitting. Then, before asking for our first witness, he said, "You will also hear evidence, either in live form or declaration, from some of the Marines or civilians who have served with Sergeant Elzie." "Terms like "among the very best Marines," "In the highest tradition of the Marine Corps," "exemplary," are terms that you will see again and again. His performance evaluations have always consistently been outstanding in each category or excellent and outstanding. He is clearly the type of Marine that this Corps should be proud of, and the fact that he said, "I am gay," should not interfere and will not interfere in his continuing to duty."

As Lanny was handing out the documents to the board he pointed out that some of them were written declarations of support from Marines and Civilians that I had worked for or with, in the Marine Corps.

Lanny Breuer: "My colleague, Lieutenant Brown, would like to read these declarations into the record."

The President of the board, Colonel Matthews: "Very well."

Major Breckenridge: "Sir, there is no reason to read them into the record given that they are in written form and available for each of the board members, to save time."

Lanny Breuer: "Mr. President and members of the board, this is an extraordinary case and we're introducing a lot of evidence that we will talk about, but we think we would like to read this into the record. It will not take more than at most ten minutes, and given what's at stake here, we feel that ten minutes is something that the board…"

Colonel Matthews: "Very well, proceed."

So Lieutenant Brown started reading from the declarations. Here are some of the statements:

"In working with Sergeant Elzie, I found his performance exemplary in all areas." "As a former Supervisor I found nothing in Sergeant Elzie's conduct which indicated his orientation in any way interfered with the satisfactory fulfillment of all duties. Sergeant Elzie's performance and behavior were above reproach and, I believe, reflected well on the Marine Corps."

"I would rank Sergeant Elzie as an outstanding Marine who

demonstrated all Marine Corps traits in an exemplary manner. Sergeant Elzie never displayed any other behavior than that of a male Marine serving out Corps. Sergeant Elzie's proficiency and conduct enhances the detachment and played an instrumental role in accomplishing its mission."

After these readings a former Sergeant whom I was stationed with on Embassy Duty testified.

Lieutenant Brown: "Would you say that Sergeant Elzie contributed positively to the security of the unit?"

Sergeant: "Yes, Sir, definitely. I believe Sergeant Elzie was an integral part of the security of the Embassy."

Lieutenant Brown: "Would you say that Sergeant Elzie was trustworthy?"

Sergeant: "Definitely, Sir, very trustworthy. I have no reason whatsoever to question Sergeant Elzie's integrity."

Lieutenant Brown: "Did you ever question his loyalty to the Marine Corps?"

Sergeant: "Not at all, sir. I believe that Sergeant Elzie is one of the most loyal Marines I have ever seen. Intense devotion to duty Corps and Country."

Lieutenant Brown: "Sergeant, generally speaking, how would you say that Sergeant Elzie performed his duties? "

Sergeant: "Outstanding Sir."

Lieutenant Brown: "And would you say that Sergeant Elzie contributed to the good order, morale and discipline of the unit with which you served with him?"

Sergeant: "As I said before, sir, Sergeant Elzie was an integral part of the Detachment in all aspects."

Lieutenant Brown went on to ask him about the living arrangements. Each Marine had his own room and there was discussion that there were shared bathroom facilities.

Lieutenant Brown: "Where was your room in relation to Sergeant Elzie's?"

Sergeant: "My room in regards to Sergeant Elzie's room, sir was approximately 25 feet way."

Lieutenant Brown: "So it would be fair to say that you saw him a great deal of the time?"

Sergeant: "On a daily basis sir."

Lieutenant Brown: "Did Sergeant Elzie ever act in any improper manner?"

Sergeant: "Sergeant Elzie never gave me any reason to question his sexuality, sir."

Lieutenant Brown: "None whatsoever?"

Sergeant: "None whatsoever."

Lieutenant Brown: "Did you ever hear any rumors?"

Sergeant: "None whatsoever, sir, and as I stated before, being such a close knit group of course we talk about each other and talk about what was going on and just on a day to day basis we are all constantly talking about each other and what is going on within the Detachment and I never heard anything to the effect of questions on Sergeant Elzie's sexual orientation."

Lieutenant Brown: "What did the other Marines think of Sergeant Elzie?"

Sergeant: "All the other Marines in the Detachment held Sergeant Elzie in very high regard. I never heard a negative thing said about Sergeant Elzie."

Lieutenant Brown: "Sergeant over the course of nine months living under the same roof, living in close conditions or close quarter, is it fair to say that perhaps, maybe a number of times you were undressed in front of Sergeant Elzie?"

Sergeant: "I can't cite a specific instance, sir, but I'm sure there were times."

Lieutenant Brown: "In fact the Marines at the Embassy shared showers didn't they?"

Sergeant: "Yes, sir, that is true. There was a communal shower facility where the vast majority of the Marines were required to shower and bath."

Lieutenant Brown: "And the Marines at the Embassy shared head facilities?"

Sergeant: "Yes, sir that is correct."

Lieutenant Brown: "And at no time did anybody to your knowledge have any problems whatsoever with Sergeant Elzie?"

Sergeant: "None whatsoever, sir."

Lieutenant Brown: "Did you ever hear of any problems with Sergeant Elzie?"

Sergeant: "No, I didn't sir."

Lieutenant Brown: "Did Sergeant Elzie ever act any differently than any other Marine at that Embassy?"

Sergeant: "No, sir he didn't. Sergeant Elzie, I would not separate, I never found anything to separate Sergeant Elzie from any other Marine in the Detachment. He was just like one of the other members of the Detachment. Nothing out of the ordinary."

Lieutenant Brown: "Did he give you any indication whatsoever as to the fact that he was gay or to his sexual orientation?"

Sergeant: "None whatsoever, sir."

Lieutenant Brown: "Did he ever give you any reason to believe or indication that he had a desire or propensity to engage in anything other than normal heterosexual activities?"

Sergeant: "No, sir, he did not."

Lieutenant Brown: "Sergeant, now that you know that Sergeant Elzie is gay and now that he has admitted to the fact in public that he is gay, would you have any problem living with him under those same conditions?"

Sergeant: "No, sir, I would not. Evidently there was not a problem living with Sergeant Elzie for the nine or ten months that I did prior. I would not have a problem living with Sergeant Elzie again. There was not a problem living with him before, I don't see why there would be now."

Lieutenant Brown: "Would you still be proud to serve and

work with him in your unit?"

Sergeant: "Yes, sir, I would."

Lieutenant Brown: "Why is that?"

Sergeant: "Because I believe Sergeant Elzie is a definite asset for the Marine Corps. He is a professional Marine; has great leadership; is a conscientious and very devoted Marine. Probably one of the best I've ever seen, sir."

Lieutenant Brown: "Has your opinion of Sergeant Elzie changed at all?"

Sergeant: "Not whatsoever, sir."

Lieutenant Brown: "One final question Sergeant. If you were back in Panama, you were back on patrol, back during the contingency operations, would you want a Marine like Sergeant Elzie in your unit with you?"

Sergeant: "Yes, sir, I would. I would definitely like a Marine of Sergeant Elzie's caliber to be with me there on patrol. Be watching my back so to speak."

Lieutenant Brown: "Why is that?"

Sergeant: "It's because of Sergeant Elzie's professionalism, his courage and his attention to detail. I know that Sergeant Elzie on patrol would be an alert member of the patrol and he would a definite asset to that patrol."

Lieutenant Brown: "Would you trust him with your life?"

Sergeant: "I would, sir."

This was the end of the questions that Lieutenant Brown had for the Sergeant. Now it was Major Breckenridge's turn. He started out asking about the background check and security checks that we went through on Embassy duty and he asked the Sergeant if those forms asked us about orientation. The fact is they didn't, and I had a "top secret" clearance. Major Breckenridge was speculating and he didn't know the answer but expected the Sergeant to know the answer to the question. If the Major would have done his due diligence he would have known that the security questionnaires don't have any questions concerning sexual orientation. He then turned to questions about living conditions.

Major Breckenridge: "All right, now let's talk about the living conditions. You indicated that you shared communal showers and that you have no problems with the actions of Sergeant Elzie. You had no knowledge at that time that he may or may not have been as of those dates a homosexual, is that right?

Sergeant: "I had no such knowledge, sir."

Major Breckenridge: "And there was nothing in his activity that indicated to you at that time that he was a homosexual?"

Sergeant: "No, sir, nothing indicated that."

Major Breckenridge: "Can you tell us with assurance that the same Marines and yourself would have felt the same serving with an openly admitted homosexual at that period of time, given that environment?"

Sergeant: "I cannot answer for the other Marines, sir, but I would not have a problem with it."

That was the end of the questions to the Sergeant by Major Breckenridge. Then the members of the board that would decide my fate asked him questions. The first was First Sergeant Goodman.

First Sergeant Goodman asked about the screening for the Embassy Duty program. There was a quick discussion about how the Marines who go to Marine Security Guard (MSG) duty are considered in the top five percent of the Marine Corps, or what some may call the "cream of the crop." They are some of the most professional Marines in the Marine Corps and MSG School is considered the hardest school in the Marine Corps due to its screening and selection process.

Then First Sergeant Goodman also proceeded to ask about the living arrangements.

First Sergeant Goodman: "And how many Marines shared rooms?"

Sergeant: "No Marines shared rooms there, sir."

First Sergeant Goodman: "No Marines shared rooms?"

Sergeant: "No, they did not, they were all individual."

First Sergeant Goodman: "Where did they shower?"

Sergeant: "Excuse me, First Sergeant?"

First Sergeant Goodman: "Where did they shower?"

Sergeant: "Two of the Marines had a communal shower, communal head facilities and the remainder of the Detachment was required to use one head facility and shower facility at the end of the hall where the rooms were."

First Sergeant Goodman: "Okay, so it wasn't as though you had a large community shower like you have here in maybe open squad bay types?

Sergeant: "No, First Sergeant, not to that effect but there were approximately seven Marines using the same shower facilities."

First Sergeant Goodman: "Not at the same time?"

Sergeant: "Of course not"

That was the end of First Sergeant Goodman's questions. The First Sergeant was trying to split hairs and because the communal bathroom didn't allow us to take showers together at the same time, the entire discussion that I had not touched any Marine was moot in their eyes because we didn't have the chance to shower together and they were trying to belittle it.

What is laughable is that there was something about this house that never came up and that was that it had a Finnish sauna and there were times when we were all in there naked. That would have been the end of the issue because I had sat in a Finnish sauna with a bunch of other guys and nothing happened. Imagine that! I guess these Marines never heard about how fireman and policeman have gays in their units and they shower together with straight men and nothing happens. And had the Finnish sauna come up it might have come out how the straight Marines used to bring women back to the Marine House and fool around with them in the Sauna.

Now there would have been some salacious details, but I am sure that these old men would have looked at that as "okay." I would have never done what they did, with a guy in the sauna.

After that line of questioning, Lieutenant Colonel Thornton, another member of the board asked the Sergeant questions.

Lieutenant Colonel Thornton: "I would also ask a question just for my own enlightenment. There is no question in my mind and we'll get it out right now that Sergeant Elzie's record is exemplary. You know that and we all know that and we can't wipe that out of our minds now. You served with him and that's a statement of fact. We have all reviewed his record and we would agree likewise. But I would ask you an honest statement now. If Sergeant Elzie had come into the Detachment and it been known at that time that he was gay or came into your squad, your infantry squad today and it was known at that time that he was gay, what would be the position that you would be confronted with, with regard to good order and discipline, cohesion and overall morale and esprit within the unit?"

Sergeant: "Well sir, answering for myself I would not have a problem with Sergeant Elzie working with me, working under me."

Lieutenant Colonel Thornton: "I didn't ask that. I said within the unit."

Sergeant: "Within the unit, sir I would see a definite problem. The average Marine today would have a problem with working with a homosexual Marine."

Lieutenant Colonel Thornton: "But the unit is in the top five percent and you still would hold that position?"

Sergeant: "I'm sorry sir; I thought the Colonel was making a generalization, not in particular to Embassy duty."

Lieutenant Colonel Thornton: "I guess my question would be, would you see it any different for those Marines in the top five percent of the Corps?"

Sergeant: "Yes sir, I would see a difference because the caliber of Marine out there is generally higher, a more mature Marine so I would say there would be a difference, sir."

Lieutenant Colonel Thornton: "What kind of difference?" Sergeant: "The more mature Marine would be more likely to accept Sergeant Elzie for a Marine and for his professionalism and Sergeant Elzie as a Sergeant of Marine and not judge him on his sexual orientation."

After listening to the questioning you might think that all of these Marines asking questions were sexually repressed, with their incessant interest in fishing for salacious details about sexual conduct and showers. As I was sitting in the court room listening to this I started thinking they must be repressed old men who were obsessed with sex. If it weren't such a serious situation it would have been laughable.

They were fishing and they wanted the information to come out slanted. It was fine that one Marine who knew me didn't have a problem with me but what about all the others? Sitting there, I wish I could have called up every Marine that I worked with to show them that the people who knew me would work with me again, but I suspect that even if I could have brought in a whole platoon of Marines they would have speculated about a dozen more that would have a problem with me. Regardless of the facts presented, they all believed that gays were incompatible with military service.

That was the end of the questioning of the Sergeant. Lanny then called a civilian employee that I had worked with on base. The questions to her centered on my performance, and again, my performance was discussed as being "outstanding." After the questioning was done, the Hearing stood at recess for lunch.

The morning so far had been hell. Even when information about how I worked well in an environment with other Marines came out the board members seemed to always want to paint a picture that because I said I was gay that could have problems. It was very frustrating and the way Major Breckenridge came across

I felt that there was no sense of fairness. This whole ordeal opened up to me the dark side of the Marine Corps. An organization that I loved was rearing its ugly side and turning on me. My headache was getting worse after lunch and I took a couple of aspirin.

After coming back from lunch, there was some discussion between the board and the attorneys about exhibits and then I read my unsworn statement to the board. Now I had done a lot of interviews up to this point and spoke in front of audiences with no problems. But with my life at stake here, while reading my statement front of the board my voice cracked. Sitting all morning and listening to people rake me over the coals was starting to get to me. I stood up and read my statement:

"I am a United States Marine. I first enlisted in the Marine Corps on November 18, 1982 and for the past eleven years, without interruption, I have served both my country and the Corps with pride, dignity and distinction. I respectfully submit this unsworn statement, pursuant to Marine Corps Separation Manual 6317.2a, in opposition to the involuntary separation proceeding that the Marine Corps has initiated against me. I originally joined the Marine Corps in 1982 for three reasons. First, I believe in the basic principles of leadership, loyalty, service, commitment, discipline, professionalism, and fitness for which the Corps stands. Second, I believe in and cherish the broader principles of liberty and democracy for which my country as a whole stands, and I greatly appreciate the special opportunity that the Marine Corps provides for me to promote and represent those principles, both at home and abroad. Third, like many sons, I admire my father, Staff Sergeant Roland Elzie, who served with honor in the United States Air Force for twenty years; I respected his commitment and service, and to a substantial degree, I wanted to follow in his footsteps."

"Since my original enlistment in 1982, the Corps has both met and exceeded my expectations, and I have responded to the call with increased dedication. Upon the expiration in 1984 of my first commitment to serve, I was honorably discharged, and I immediately reenlisted for active duty. Upon the expiration in 1991 of my second commitment to serve, I again was honorably discharged, and again I immediately reenlisted. My current commitment will expire in November 1995. If allowed to continue my service, I would be eligible to reenlist once again at that point and, under current guidelines, I believe that I would be eligible to retire with full benefits in 1997, having served as a career Marine."

"My dedication has not been unvalued; the Marine Corps has appreciated and rewarded my service. My previous discharges have been honorable; my immediate reenlistments encouraged and accepted enthusiastically. More significantly, I have been commended for several distinctions and achievements."

"For example, in 1982, I received a meritorious promotion to the rank of Private First Class (PFC) after completing boot camp in San Diego. In 1983, I received a second meritorious promotion to the rank of Corporal while serving as an active reservist in a Marine Air Control Squadron (MACS) in Denver. While in Denver, I also served part-time as a Marine Corps recruiter, where my achievements provoked a request that I enroll in informal training for full time recruiters. I declined that request to return to active duty, and shortly thereafter, I was transferred to the Marine Corps Air Station at Cherry Point, North Carolina."

"In 1985, I received a citation for "outstanding service" from Lieutenant Colonel Chevalier, my commanding officer at Cherry Point. In his citation, Lieutenant Colonel Chevalier recognized me as "an essential element in maintaining the professionalism and effective function" of the program to which I had been assigned. I was commended for "outstanding results," "versatility and flexibility," and "proficient accomplishment." In closing, the citation stated:

"your competence and initiative in seeking and accepting additional responsibilities far exceeded that of your contemporaries. You have consistently set the example as a Marine NCO by your unselfish attitude, dedication, and performance as a leader of Marines. Your performance is in keeping with the highest tradition of the United States Marine Corps."

"Later that same year, I received a Certificate of Commendation from Brigadier General James M. Mead, Commanding General of the Cherry Point Air Station, for "superior performance of duty" during the fifteen month period that I was stationed there, from July 1984 through September 1985. In his citation, General Mead commended me for "exceptional drive and technical expertise," for "tireless efforts and enthusiasm," and for "professional skill and loyal dedication to duty that reflect great credit up me, the Cherry Point Command, and the United States Marine Corps."

"Similarly, in 1988, I received a Navy Achievement Medal in a citation signed by the Secretary of the Navy. This medal acknowledged "professional achievement" during the twenty month tour of duty from October 1985 until May 1987 that I served in Guantanamo, Bay Cuba, where I was stationed immediately following my service at Cherry Point."

"In 1989 I was nominated by my battalion command in Okinawa, Japan for "Marine of the Year" honors. After my nomination, I then was selected Marine of the Year both for my battalion, the Third Medical Battalion, and for my group, the Third Force Service Support Group. On previous occasions and at previous locations, I had been selected as Marine of the Quarter (for third quarter of 1986) and NCO of the Quarter (for the third and fourth quarters of 1988).

"In 1989, I also was accepted into and attended the Marine Security Guard (MSG) School at Quantico, Virginia. Unlike approximately one-half of the class, whom the Corps routinely drops from the program, I successfully completed that program in July 1989, whereupon I was posted to the United States Embassy in Helsinki,

Finland. Later during the "Helsinki Summit" between Presidents Bush and Gorbachev, I was entrusted with the security of some of our most senior government officers, including then Secretary of State James A. Baker, National Security Advisor Brent Scowcroft, and White House Chief of Staff John Sununu."

"In September 1990 upon completion of my embassy service in Helsinki, Ambassador John Giffen Weinmann kindly commended me for "showing fine leadership qualities on the job as well as a refreshing eagerness to learn about Finland, our host country." He acknowledged that I have a "can-do attitude which is clearly visible to all who deal with me on a professional level," and he stated that I am "reliable, hard working, and enthusiastic in any task I undertake." In closing, he concluded that I am "most definitely prepared for a position of greater responsibility," and he surmised that I have "a very positive future ahead."

"Mr. William J. Burke, Counselor of the Embassy for Administrative Affairs, similarly acknowledged my "professionalism," "maturity," "intellectual curiosity," and "outstanding on the job performance," and he too recommended me "for positions of greater responsibility."

"In addition to the foregoing commendations, I have received several decorations for good conduct and achievement over the course of my military career. These include, among others, a Good Conduct Medal (GCM), four Overseas Ribbons (OSRs), a Meritorious Unit Citation (MUC), A Sea Service Deployment Ribbon (SSDR), a Southwest Asia Ribbon (SWA), and a National Defense Service medal (NDSM). In addition, I have a Rifle Expert Badge as a certified expert with the M-16, and I am a certified pistol expert with the .357 Magnum."

"Moreover, my performance evaluations have been consistently positive throughout my career. In fact, in my latest evaluation, on January 7, 1993, my performance was rated as "excellent" or "outstanding" in all applicable categories, and I was adjudged "qualified for promotion." In addition, in response to a standard form question asking the evaluator to "consider the requirements of service in war" and to "indicate his or her attitude toward having this Marine under your command," I was rated as "particularly desired." In the space provided for written remarks, I was described in the following terms:

- "Highly efficient and of noteworthy reliability"Eager to learn new skills and techniques"
- "Demonstrated ability and desire to progress"
- "Highly productive"
- "Able to remain stable and composed when job requirements rose above normal, compounded by staffing shortages"
- "Displayed confidence in own abilities that proved motivational to others"
- "Provided timely completion of demanding requirements"
- "Great growth potential"
- "Will make excellent career Marine"

"During the week of January 24, 1993, less than three weeks after this most recent performance evaluation, a team from ABC Nightly News came to visit Camp Lejeune to conduct interviews for a television news story about homosexuality in the military. I agreed to be interviewed. During the course of my interview, which occurred on January 29, 1993, I admitted publicly for the first time in my life that I am gay.

"Unlike other gay and lesbian service members who have admitted their homosexuality in news interviews, I did not elect to conceal my name, to disguise my voice, or to hide my face behind a screen or in a purposefully-cast shadow. Although I certainly understand and respect the decisions of those who have masked themselves, I am proud of my record and of who I am. After some vexing thought, therefore, I agreed to make my identity known. I do not believe that a homosexual should be required to conceal his or her identity like a mob informant. I have done nothing wrong; I believe I should fear no reprisal.

"In addition, I was emboldened in my decision to admit that I am gay by the reassuring statements of our new Commander in Chief, President Clinton, who indicated an intention to lift the ban on military service by qualified homosexuals.

"On the night of January 29, 1993, the ABC Nightly News with Peter Jennings ran a story on homosexuality in the military as its lead story. Among other things, the program aired the portion of the videotaped interview in which I admitted that I am gay."

"On February 5, 1993, I was informed orally by my battalion commanding officer, Colonel Kahl, that an application that I had submitted in December 1992 under the Voluntary Separation Incentive and Special Separation Benefit (VSI/SSB) program had been approved. As I understand it, the VSI/SSB program was established by the Pentagon to scale down the size of the armed services in the wake of the Persian Gulf and Cold Wars. Through the program, qualified Marines may receive early retirement and still be entitled to full pension, medical and veterans benefits."

"On February 10, 1993, I was informed by Colonel Kahl that, as a result of the admission of my sexual orientation and continued public remarks relating to that admission, I would not receive a VSI/SSB discharge but rather would be given two other options:

(a) voluntary discharge without entitlement to full benefits or (b) involuntary separation under Marine Corps Separation Manual 6207. I declined to accept a voluntary discharge. Later that same day I received a Notification of Separation Proceedings from my company commander, Major Rook, informing me of his intention to recommend to the Commanding General that I be discharged pursuant to Marine Corps Separation Manual 6207 "by reason of my admittance to being a homosexual."

133

"On February 18, 1993, Colonel Kahl again counseled me regarding my VSI/SSB request. He advised me that, under the VSI/SSB program, I could elect to accept a release from active duty and be transferred to the standby reserve, pursuant to current White House directives, pending a further Executive Order regarding my eligibility for continued military service. This apparent offer bore two conditions. First, it was conditioned upon my agreement to waive any right to my initial VSI/SSB payment, which ordinarily would be paid on the date of my release from active duty. Second, and more importantly, it was conditioned on the contingency that the ultimate Executive decision would not render me ineligible for continue military service; if that ultimate decision were to render me ineligible, I could be discharged without any VSI/SSB benefits. I declined to accept this conditional VSI/SSB offer. Accordingly, the current involuntary separation proceedings have proceeded."

"I oppose these proceedings. I am at a loss to understand how the mere and honest admission that I am gay can provide a rational basis for my involuntary discharge. I do not understand why that admission is relevant and how it can affect and, indeed, eviscerate the record of service and achievement that I have built over the past eleven years. I do not believe that my sexual status is pertinent to my performance as a Marine."

"The Marine Corps in which I enlisted and in which I proudly have served for over a decade cherishes and promotes leadership and loyalty. It rewards honesty, discipline, professionalism, and commitment. It protects the people in whom it invests, and it never abandons a good soldier or leaves one behind. I believe that I possess and have demonstrated the qualities of a good soldier. I am proud to be a Marine, and I wish to continue to serve with pride and without any hint of shame. I respectfully oppose my involuntary separation."

"Executed on this 31st day of March 1993, Sergeant Justin C. Elzie, USMC."

It took me about five minutes to read my statement to the court. There was some discussion between the board and the attorneys about the exhibits and my statements to the press. Then

the President of the Board, Colonel Matthews, called for a recess before they began summation.

After the recess the most unusual thing happened in the courtroom. Major Breckenridge tried to pull a fast one.

Major Breckenridge: "Mr. President (Colonel Matthews), I have a somewhat unusual request to make. During the recess, I was approached by an individual who I had never met before by the name of Holly Koerber who is a lawyer in Jacksonville who I noticed had been sitting in the proceedings room observing the proceedings. She was recently on the panel here in Jacksonville, North Carolina, which discussed homosexuals in the military and was responsible for setting up a number of the panel members and so forth that come forward. During the recess, she represented to me that she had pertinent information for this board regarding the length of time that Sergeant Elzie has been engaged in, at least, contacts with other homosexuals, including while at the embassy; that he is the president of a local homosexual organization here in this area; and we would ask the opportunity to present that evidence to the board."

Colonel Matthews: "Counsel?"

Lanny Breuer: "Mr. President, board members, this is an outrageous request and I want to reflect our strenuous opposition. First of all, this witness has been sitting in this room the entire time and the Separation Manual explicitly states that witnesses shall not be in the room. So, that's the first point: This witness has been here the entire time. Second of all this very witness stated to me earlier that though she is a lawyer, she also considers herself to be a journalist and that she had invited Sergeant Elzie to participate in some sort of forum. Now, "homosexual conduct" means sexual homosexual conduct. It does not mean speaking to people

135

who are gay. We all speak to people who are gay. And if Major Breckenridge now in rebuttal is going to introduce a witness who's simply going to say that Sergeant Elzie speaks with people who are gay, that is nothing but an infringement on his First Amendment rights. It's entirely irrelevant. The only thing that this shows is the utter weakness of the government's case. "

"It goes to what I said before. This person who is a partisan, this woman has disclosed that she is very much against the ban, against removing the ban, is in the forefront of removing the ban, is one of the people in the forefront of this political issue. Clearly at some point, she now has gone up to Major Breckenridge. Whatever information she had, Colonel, she had a long time ago. Whatever information she had about Justin Elzie, she knew. She knew about this hearing and through one way or another, she clearly got permission from someone on the base."

"It's entirely improper now for her to be called. And what is she going to say? She's going to according to the proffer of Major Breckenridge; I don't know this woman, she is going to say that Sergeant Elzie deals with people who are homosexual. We all talk to people who are homosexual, whether we know it or not."

"This case is about status and, as desperate as the government is, it hasn't changed one bit. And, homosexual conduct does not mean losing your First Amendment rights. This is just another reflection of what happened yesterday when Sergeant Elzie's roommate was rounded up. It's highly improper. We vehemently object to it. It is not rebuttal. The Major has closed his case. I am not in any way implying that the Major has done anything improper. I completely take, as an officer of the court, his representation that this witness has just approached him. But, this witness's testimony would be highly improper. It would do nothing more than to make this a political forum and it would do nothing other than to chill the First Amendment rights of people. It has nothing to do with conduct, which they have failed to prove. And, talking to people

136

is not homosexual conduct. Being an activist is not homosexual conduct, whether you like it or not. And so, I vehemently object to that. And, with that I think I have made my record." Colonel Matthews: "Legal advisor?"

Major Hammond: "Sir, I think it is as Major Breckenridge has pointed out; it is very unusual for him to make this request at this point in time, since everybody has closed their evidence. I think it is a good point that Lanny Breuer has made that, in fact, this person has sat in and heard the entire evidence throughout the hearing. And again, given the circumstances around it, I do not think that it would be a good idea to have that witness come in, sir."

Colonel Matthews: "I would agree. Again, I can't as I understand the regulations for separation, a separation board cannot preclude evidence from being submitted, but it will be my recommendation, Major Breckenridge, that it isn't appropriate. You desire to call, I can't as I understand it, legally cannot stop the major from calling the witness."

Major Hammond: "Yes, you may sir."

Colonel Matthews: "Then I would. Because I think it would be prejudicial to the fair hearing that is to be conducted. Furthermore, I would indicate that if the purpose of that is to present evidence regarding the length of time that Sergeant Elzie has been involved with this association or whatever, by his own admission in the newspaper articles, there's testimony to that effect."

Major Breckenridge: "Yes, sir. I appreciate the court's ruling and the fact that the board will not consider her testimony. We do have the opportunity to attach items to the record, which were not considered, to the board and we would ask leave of the board to attach a statement by her after the board has closed its deliberation."

Colonel Matthews: "Was that statement made before these proceedings or as a result of sitting in here and hearing what had occurred here throughout the day?"

Major Breckenridge: "Well, her testimony does not change by

the fact that she heard other evidence. This would, these are all conversations that she had with individuals two to three weeks ago, sir."

Lanny Breuer: "It is no less inappropriate whether it is live testimony or attached to the record, it goes to the exact same point. This is a witness who, for whatever reason, feels that the government's case, which she is an outspoken ally of, isn't going well. It's nothing but a desperate attempt. And whether you call it "attaching it to the record," putting it in writing, it makes no difference. We vehemently object. The Major has closed his case. We have closed our case. We're ready for final argument and we're going to ask you to rely on the evidence before you. She is going to say nothing. Once more, the proffer is nothing even remotely relevant. It simply goes to contact with homosexuals according to this woman. I vehemently, vehemently object."

Colonel Matthews: "Legal advisor?"

Major Hammond: "Sir, without her testimony of course this board cannot consider it. Therefore I think it would be wise not to have her testimony. If there is some other process where the government can listen to this kind of evidence or attach this kind of evidence the so be it. But it will not come before this board and will not be attached to the record of these proceedings today, sir."

At this a couple members of the board asked for a short recess so that they could discuss and vote on it. After the recess, Colonel Matthews announced their decision.

Colonel Matthews: "The board, in closed session, has voted unanimously that to admit this testimony would violate the procedures. It would be unfair and inappropriate for the oral or written testimony to be admitted."

At long last, the final arguments began. Then the board went into recess at 1500 hours for deliberations. I got up and walked out into the hall with my attorneys. It was sunny out and I couldn't help but take note of how hospital-like the waiting area was, with

138

its extremely-white walls, uncomfortable furniture, and bad coffee.

I had a really bad headache by this time and so I just wanted to lie down. I had never felt so alone or beaten up in my life as I had at that point. I just sat down and put my head in my hands. At 1651 hours the board was called back into session.

Colonel Matthews: "The board has considered all of the testimony and evidence introduced by the recorder and the counsel for the respondent in this matter. The board considers at the heat of this matter the DOD directive and the Marine Corps Order. The basis paragraph in the DOD directive number 1332.14, and the policy paragraph in Marine Corps Order P1921.6, specifically paragraph 6207.1 both address the presence of servicemembers who, by conduct or statement emphasis statement demonstrate a propensity to engage in homosexual conduct are seriously impairing the accomplishment of the military mission by affecting the good order and discipline."

"According, the DOD Directive and Marine Corps Order, as written, determined the board's deliberations."

"Therefore, based upon his own public admission and numerous media statements, Sergeant Elzie is found to be homosexual. Based upon common sense and reason, it is the board's opinion that admission of homosexuality affects good order and discipline."

"Further, by his own public admission, Sergeant Elzie has admitted that his acknowledgement of being homosexual has affected good order and discipline."

"Thus, the board finds that the evidence presented does support the allegations sent forth in the Notice of Proposed Separation."

"The board finds that separation is warranted in this case with respect to the reason for separation set forth in the Notice of Proposed Separation."

"The board makes no additional finds. The board recommends discharge. The board recommends the general and specific

139

basis for separation to be homosexual admissions."

"Based on testimony received regarding Sergeants Elzie's exemplary service, the board recognizes that and accordingly recommends honorable characterization of service."

The board adjourned at 1654 hours.

As soon as the board adjourned I just wanted to get out of the courtroom. I was tired but there were a lot of news media outside and so when we walked out the door I did a couple of interviews. I told them that the board had acknowledged that I was an exemplary Marine but based on my statements that I was gay that was enough to discharge me. They had taken statements that I had said that some people giving me the cold shoulder at work as evidence that it affected good order and discipline, however they ignored the statements I had also said that some people were starting to loosen up and I had had several people that came to give me encouragement. They also ignored the Sergeant who I had worked with and his testimony. Now what would happen is that after reviews of the findings it would then be up to the Secretary of the Navy to decide what to do next but in the mean time I would be going back to work and just wait on the decision.

When I spoke to the media I kept an upbeat exterior, but down deep inside my being I was tired, frustrated and disappointed in the Marine Corps that I loved so much.

I was quoted in the US News & Report magazine as saying, "I thought through it all it had been worth coming out. Because I had shown my fellow Marines with whom I had trained and worked with and showered with for years that gays can be good Marines." I also pointed out that aside from my case there were other cases in the military where Marines and sailors were openly gay and that a lot of times commanders have not turned in these people. "What I have noticed is, on a one to one basis they don't give a damn."

My one final statement that day to the press was really how I felt inside, but it was also somewhat prophetic. "It's definitely not a good decision, and it's only the beginning."

I walked out of the building and back over to the legal building with my attorneys. After saying some goodbyes I head for home. I really felt down and out at that point. After sitting there all day and listening to people lie and trying to ruin my credibility and character was very taxing. This was the worst day of my life. I got home and John was already there.

As John sat on the couch I briefed him on the day's events. After I explained everything to him, the enormity of what had happened that day hit me like a ton of bricks. I walked over to the couch and broke down in his arms. All I could say to him was that I couldn't believe how hateful people could be. Why does God allow people to be so hateful? I couldn't understand why I was the only Marine to come out and fight this bigoted and hateful policy. I had hoped when I came out that others in the Marine Corps would follow me, but they didn't. Was I the only Marine who felt this way? Why had others not also stepped forward? Was I the only one with courage and drive to stand up for what was right? Sadly, the answer came back as "yes."

I was the sacrificial Marine. I had stood up for what was morally right and what our founding fathers had talked about, liberty and justice. I now would pay the price for my passionate patriotism, integrity and moral call of duty to stand up for ethical principles. At that moment I realized that as the Marine Corps was trying to make an example out of me that I was going to be the only Marine to stand up. I needed to pick myself up, brush myself off and continue the fight and carry on. Silence breeds injustice and as Harvey Milk once said: "Rights are won only by those who make their voices heard."

I would continue to carry the torch.

CHAPTER 14
SENATE HEARINGS

0930 hours 3 April 1993 Camp Lejeune, North Carolina

Aristotle wrote: "Whereas the law is passionless, passion must ever sway the heart of man."

If you talked to any of my friends, one of the words that they would use to describe me is "passionate." Sitting on the couch that Saturday morning watching television and getting ready to go out to get coffee and the paper, I wondered whether having such deep passion about fighting injustice in our society was a curse. I had dived right into this with the most fervent passion and drive and look where I was: about ready to be kicked out of the Marines, with an uncertain future, ostracized like a leper by a lot of the people I met, and not sure if I was changing any minds on the subject of gays in the military. It didn't look like I was inspiring anyone to follow in my footsteps. Whenever I started thinking of just being quiet, going way and throwing away my passion, depression took over and the feeling that there was no reason to live would be the most prevalent—because if I couldn't make a difference in people's lives, then there was no reason to live.

I looked at my options. On the one hand, keep charging. On the other, go away and watch my soul die. That morning I picked myself back up again and knew that I had to keep charging.

So I got up off the couch and went out to get a paper. On the front page was a story about Friends Lounge. Thursday night, the night following my discharge hearing, three Molotov cocktails had been hurled at the bar while the place was packed. They ignited the side of the building and the surrounding woods. Three men dressed in black with military haircuts, were spotted running from the scene. They were still at large.

After my Administrative Discharge Board proceedings, the results were sent to several Congressional offices that had been tracking my case, and a couple which had helped my attorneys with information for the case. Congressman Gerry Studds, Congressman Barney Frank, Congresswoman Patricia Schroeder, Congressman Craig Thomas, Senator Alan Simpson, and Senator Ted Kennedy were all on the list.

Richard Avedon's gay military servicemembers photo shoot, with me and my six compatriots ran on April 5 in The New Yorker magazine. The article, alongside the photos titled: "Liberating Forces," mentioned how Clinton had just had his first press conference and how his comments showed he was backtracking on the removal of the ban on gays in the military. David Mixner, a prominent gay rights activist and friend of President Clinton, was quoted in the article saying, "We may have placed too much faith and trust in someone who doesn't share our own passion for our own freedom." Right around this time the Pentagon was floating options, one of which was segregating gays in the military. The article also mentioned that the next night after the press conference, David Mixner had gone on ABC Nightline to state that segregating gays "is morally wrong, it is repugnant, it is something that we cannot accept."

On Saturday, April 10 I made the trip up to Raleigh, North Carolina to speak at a Campaign for Military Service's "Tour of Duty" rally. The Campaign for Military Service was a short-term, broad-based effort to secure congressional and public support for President Clinton's proposal to issue an executive order eliminating the ban against gay men, lesbians and bisexuals in the U.S. Military. The Campaign for Military Service was brought together and organized by Tom Stoddard. The bus tour was going around to different cities, talking about the issue of gays in the military, and had veterans on the tour, like Tanya Domi and Alan Stephens, speaking out. Going up to Raleigh right after my discharge hearing and talking to other veterans was an energizing experience.

Two weeks later, on Friday, April 23, John and I packed the car and drove up to Washington, D.C. for the 1993 "March on Washington". That weekend there were a lot of activities in D.C. One of the things going on was the AIDS Quilt was being displayed on the D.C. Mall. John and I went to see it because I was trying to find military friends who had died of AIDS. While we were walking around the Quilt I unexpectedly ran into an old friend, Brain Lighty, whom I had known while I was stationed at Cherry Point. We hadn't seen each other in ten years. That weekend John and I both marched in the Parade. John wore camouflage face paint to keep from him being recognized. At the huge rally on the mall all of the military servicemembers who had come out all went up on stage. There was Joseph Steffan, Keith Meinhold, Tracy Thorne, Gretta Cammermeyer, Tom Pannicca, Zoe Dunning, Jose Zuniga, myself, and others.

It was a great weekend for John and I to get away and relax a bit after all that we had been through so far.

During this time the Senate Armed Service Committee was starting to hold hearings on gays in the military. The Campaign For Military Service, with permission and encouragement from my attorneys had asked me to testify. I took off for D.C. on the weekend of May 8, and stayed with friends in D.C., and prepared to meet my attorneys on Monday and then testify at the Senate Armed Services Committee Hearings on Tuesday, May 11.

On Tuesday I went up to Capitol Hill with my attorneys and filed in with the rest of the crowd into the committee hearing room and took a seat right behind the table. They were having several people testify against lifting the ban first. The first group included: Army General Norman Schwarzkopf, retired, USMC Colonel Fred

Peck, Navy Command Master Chief David Borne and USMC Major Kathleen Bergeron. After their testimony our group got seated at the table to testify. In our group were Army National Guard Colonel Margarethe Cammemeyer, Chief Petty Officer Steve Amidon, Air Force Staff Sergeant Thomas Paniccia, and myself. They had us all read our statements and then they had questions for us. It was an interesting day, answering questions from Senators like Strom Thurmond and Sam Nunn, both of whom were against lifting the ban. When I got ready to read my statement I was surprised at how calm I was. I didn't think about how many people were watching because if I had I probably would have been pretty nervous!

My Senate Hearings Statement:

"Mr. Chairman and Members of the Committee, my name is Justin Elzie. I am a Sergeant currently on active duty in the United States Marine Corps stationed at Camp Lejeune, North Carolina."

"First, I want to thank you for giving me the opportunity to speak to you all on this tremendously important issue. I would also like you to know, at the outset, that I am the subject of pending administrative discharge proceedings on account of my statements that I am gay. I have asked that a copy of the transcript from my administrative discharge hearing, which occurred this past March 31st, be entered into the record, along with a copy of the personal statement that I submitted at that hearing."

"I am from Cheyenne, Wyoming, and I grew up on a farm there. I was in the Boy Scouts, wrestled in high school, and was named in Who's Who Among American High School Students. My dad was in the Air Force for twenty years, and like many young Americans, I wanted to follow in my father's footsteps. I joined the Marine Corps in 1982. I went to boot camp in San Diego, California, held a leadership position, and was meritoriously promoted upon graduation. Throughout my career, I have been stationed on the east and west coasts of the US, as well as in Japan, Cuba, Europe, and most recently, in the Middle East during Desert Storm."

"Every step of the way, I have received awards and commendations for my outstanding service to my country. For example, while stationed in Okinawa, Japan in 1988, I competed for and received the honor of Marine of the Year for my battalion. I then went on to compete for and did receive the same honor, Marine of the Year, for the 3rd FSSG, which is approximately eight battalions of Marines including my own."

"In 1989, I went through a rigorous screening process and completed the Marine Corps Embassy Guard School in Quantico, Virginia. Out of the class, only fifty percent of us graduated. Marine Embassy Guards are considered the top ten percent of the Marines, the elite. As a Marine Embassy Guard, you see and screen every person that comes into the American Embassy. The Marine Embassy Guard has the keys to the American Embassy and is the first line of defense in protecting our embassies. Marines are considered diplomats. We represent not only the Marine Corps but the United States of America."

"While on embassy duty, I stood guard at the Bush-Gorbachev summit in Helsinki, Finland. I was responsible during my shift for the safety of secretary of State Jim Baker, National Security Advisor Brent Scowcroft, and the top staff. During Desert Storm, I served at the American Consulate in Alexandria, Egypt. I was the Assistant Detachment Commander for the Marines there. I remember handling many difficult and serous security situations that could have been an embarrassment to the United States and a danger to the lives of the American staff. At those times, the American Ambassador and Consulate General congratulated me for a job well done."

"Despite my outstanding accomplishments, I know that if I had uttered three words, "I am gay," then I would instantly have gone from an outstanding Marine to a deficient Marine in the eyes of the Marine Corps, though not in the eyes of my fellow Marines or the State Department. I could be the best Marine in the Marines, save the lives of my platoon, and even die for my country, but because I am gay, no matter how good I am, I can never be good enough. I wonder if I am sent to Bosnia soon and die, what is the Marine Corps going to tell my parents?"

"Since publicly stating my sexual orientation, I have had former peers, Marines, and State Department employees from embassy duty write letters of support for me. I remember receiving letters from Americans during Christmas when I was in Egypt, and their comments to us that they were proud of us serving our country overseas gave me a great feeling. I also felt that great feeling the night the ground war started. I was on duty that night, and as I walked through the Consulate listening to the BBC, many thoughts went through my mind. I was praying for my fellow service men and women in Saudi Arabia and knowing that at any moment, I could receive a bomb threat at the Consulate. But I was prepared to handle that and if need be, to die for my country. My performance evaluations while on embassy duty for three years were nothing less than outstanding."

"For the past year, I have been stationed in Camp Lejeune, North Carolina. I watched this past year the brave women come forward and talk about the harassment and discrimination surrounding Tailhook. I also witnessed fellow servicemen and women describing the discrimination suffered by gays and lesbians in the military. As an American who believes in the ideals of liberty and justice for all, and that all people are created equal, I could stay silent no longer. I am here today as a United States Marine who supports the lifting of the ban."

"On January 29th of this year, I announced to an interviewer from ABC World News Tonight that I am gay. I made this announcement to make a positive difference and to tell the public about the many gays and lesbians in the military who are doing an outstanding job. As a matter of fact, I know many service members whose peers know are gay and whose commanders know are gay, but nothing is done about it because it is not a problem. These servicemembers are not doing any misconduct, are not causing bad morale, and are an essential part of their units. It is ironic that I received my performance evaluation for the past year on the day I publicly stated I am gay, and my superiors said that I would make an excellent career Marine.

"Senator Nunn, sir, I was watching C-SPAN this last week and heard you say to Senator Feinstein that everybody in testifying to the committee was talking in generalities and giving no specifics about how to carry out lifting the ban. Sir, you asked what are we going to tell the officers, the petty officers, the sergeants. Well, sir, I am not General Schwarzkopf, and I did not command all the troops in Operation Desert Storm, but as a highly honored NCO who has led Marines, I have some suggestions.

"Number one: People need to support the chain of command. Sir, as a Marine, I am taught to follow orders. If the order comes down to lift the ban, the NCO's in the Marines that I know can carry out the orders and handle it, regardless of personal feelings. So Number one, support the chain of command.

"Number two: Lay the law down that the Marine Corps will not tolerate discrimination based on sexual orientation, just like we do not tolerate racism or sexism in the military. This last year I had one of my Marines telling racist jokes and making racist statements in the office. I pulled that Marine aside and made it clear not only to him but to the whole office that I would not tolerate racist language, that we were here to do a job and this kind of talk only undermines unit cohesion and hurts the mission. From there on out, I heard no more racist talk.

"I see right now sir, the same thing happening with the anti-gay talk in the military today. It is hurting morale. The Marine Corps is very diverse, African Americans, Hispanics, women, gays and lesbians. By spreading prejudice and intolerance of other people's ideas, worth, beliefs, and human dignity, we are going against everything we have been striving for, and we are only shooting ourselves in the foot. The solution is education and leadership. So Number two: we do not tolerate discrimination period.

"Number three: Clear and strict rules of conduct need to be enforced fairly and equally for everyone. Straight across the board. Sexual harassment is sexual harassment; misconduct is misconduct, whether you are straight or gay.

"So, in answer to your question, Senator Nunn, it can be done. NCO's can understand these three points and command the men and women under them accordingly: #1, people need to support the chain of command; #2, lay the law down that the military will not tolerate discrimination based on sexual orientation; and #3, clear and strict rules of conduct need to be enforced fairly and equally for everyone.

"Since I publicly stated that I am gay, I have had an administrative discharge hearing. A board of Marine Corps officers explicitly found at that hearing that I am an "exemplary" Marine, but because I said three words, "I am gay", they recommended that I be discharged from the Marine Corps.

"Frequently, people come up to me who recognize me and make the comment that they think what the Marine Corps is doing to me is wrong and that they support me. Nine times out of ten that person is an African American, woman, or Hispanic."

"I have realized as you did yesterday, Mr. Chairman that a lot of service members do not really mind serving with gays and lesbians because they know they already do. A lot of Marines are afraid to come forward and say how they feel because their careers could be damaged. If you stick a microphone or a camera in a Marine's or sailor's face and ask them how they feel on this subject, chances are that no matter what their personal beliefs, they will stick to the party line and support the ban. That is what the chain of command promotes, and they are afraid of being labeled as gay themselves. There is a fear of guilt by association."

"In closing, I ask you all to judge me as those who know me best have judged me, as a professional. I have won the admiration of those with who I have served. As one heterosexual Marine, a Marine who has faced enemy fire, testified at my discharge hearing, if he were ever to face such fire again, he would want me to be there his side. Senators, being a Marine means being a Marine first, regardless of sexual orientation. Thank you.

After my testimony there were a lot of questions for us all. Some of the press would later compare my testimony with that of the Marine Major Kathleen Bergeron. One article was titled: "Marines of two minds on scrapping gay ban." They said, "a pair of dedicated Marines squared off Tuesday with conflicting views on the proposed lifting of the ban on homosexuals in the armed forces." The Major testified that "in my opinion, any attempt to assimilate homosexuals into the Marine Corps will undermine and eventually destroy the small unit cohesion that is the critical ingredient for the Marine Corps as a fight force."

I on the other hand was a living example of a gay Marine having worked in small units where there was no destruction of the morale or unit cohesion. I also pointed out that I knew many service members whose peers knew they were gay and there were no problems in their units. I was hoping that people could get past their prejudices and see that we had facts on our side and they had assumptions and fears. At the end of the day I felt hopeful that I had at least made some difference, but I wasn't sure.

When I got back to North Carolina from that weekend I started having mail pour in from people who had seen my testimony at the Senate Hearings. Up to now I had gotten a fair amount of mail but now it really started coming. The majority was positive but there would be once in a while negative ones or ones that didn't agree with lifting the ban. For example during my testimony at the Senate Hearings I was asked by Senator Nunn, "Did you consider the impact of your coming out would have on the moral issue?"

My answer was; "I think it's morally right and the way God made me." That comment struck a nerve with a lot of people and generated more mail than I could have imagined. A couple of "Christians" who wrote me tried to say that the God condemned me and that homosexuality was vile and an abomination and that it was not genetic. These letters didn't affect me as I grew up learning the Bible and knew that Jesus never said anything about homosexuality. I felt I had an understanding with God about why he had made me this way and it wasn't wrong. I of course also sometimes got one or two letters that were even more "out there" in their homophobic language and bigoted hate, if saying I was an abomination wasn't enough! One was pretty bombastic from a former Marine and kind of floored me when I read it. This former Marine, when he addressed the outside of the envelope he put after my name, the word "faggot" on the envelope. Here is his letter in its entirety with all the caps and punctuation that he used:

Mr. Justin Elzie,

> *You are a DISGRACE to the USMC, and I hope by the time you get this, your butt will be out of the Corps! You forget one thing asshole you LIED when you enlisted!*
> *And if you think "Embassy Guards" are "the elite of the Corps," you are FULL OF SHIT!! You are a man (and I use the word lightly!) who LIED to get into my Marine Corps. To me and 99% of the Corps you are SCUM! Sodomy is also a crime under the UCMJ, and I hope they hang your sorry ass!!*
> *You have DISGRACED that uniform and embarrassed every true Marine who ever lived! For that I hope you die of rectal cancer, butt fucker! God, how repugnant! What about "In God we trust," or "GOD, country, Corps!"? HUH? You're not a Marine, you are a phony!*

Fuck You!

Semper Fi!
Jim

Even though these few letters were pretty hateful, the number and stories of the positive ones clearly outshone the negative ones and at times really moved my heart. There was one friend who sent me messages from a Prodigy bulletin board online from many people expressing support. I also got letters from numerous gay military servicemembers in the closet who were worried about their careers. I got letters from a Rabbi of a Jewish congregation, as well as a Sergeant Major in the Canadian Army and a Commander in the Dutch Army who both pointed out that gays could serve openly in their militaries and I was welcome to join them if I wanted to. A mother of a gay doctor who wrote me and thanked me for being who I was and coming forward and wanted to match me up with her gay son. I got a letter from a straight military wife of a Marine who said my coming out helped make the point to her husband who was less than open-minded about the issue. I got a letter from a young gay man in Colorado who said, "The second reason I have for writing is to thank you. By openly coming forward you've given me the courage to finally face my own sexuality. Your example of courage and honesty have helped me face the final step in my process of coming out. If you can face public scrutiny and the loss of your career, certainly I can face my future. I understand now the freedom and release you spoke of."

Two other letters that really made an impact on me were a letter that I got from a twenty-seven year-old firefighter and teacher from North Carolina who spoke about his rejection from his parents and how, because of my story, he was planning on speaking about my plight to his ninth-grade class. He said, "Perhaps your shining example, though it may not seem so, can endure in a young student's mind as a story of sincere courage, one to be respected." The other letter I got was from a seventy-six year-old grandmother from Kalamazoo, Michigan that reduced me to tears. Her letter was amazing in giving me encouragement to carry on. She wrote, "Don't spend time answering this. Just take a walk and continue to reflect on your determination to correct a great wrong. Maintain your courage, knowing that you're doing the right thing. Remember "if it should be, it can be.

At times it was the letters that I got that helped encourage me to keep going.

Little Cowboy in 1963. 6 months old and my Dad showing me how to sit in a saddle. This is one of my favorite pictures of me and my Dad.

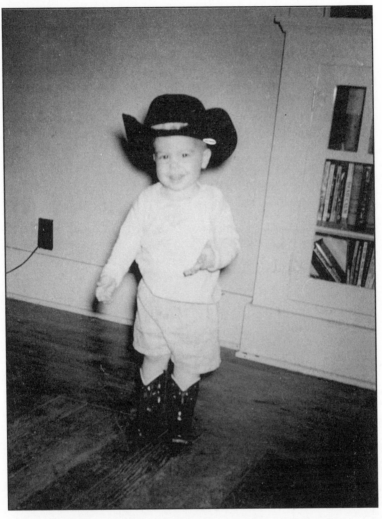

Little Cowboy in 1965. 3 years of age wearing my cowboy boots
and my Dads cowboy hat.

Little Cowboy in May 1964. I am holding my little sister, Becky, who was 3 months old. This is my favorite picture with my little sister. I now had a playmate!

Above. Little Cowboy in 1963. On a donkey, you notice I have a seat belt on so I don't fall out of the saddle. 1971 my 9th Birthday. *Left,* This is the only birthday that I remember as a kid and it was special because I got a brand new bike.

One of my high school photos. I wish I still had that shirt.

San Diego 1982. My Boot Camp photo.

Young Marine stationed at MCAS Cherry Point. Here with my best friend then, Len Regan.

1988 Okinawa Japan. This is a photo taken of me to go before a board. I was chosen as "Marine of the Year" for 3rd FSSG.

1989, Taken at my Marine Embassy Guard Graduation at Quantico VA. Here I am with the Commandant of the Marine Corps at the time, General Gray. I am proud to have met him twice in my career.

1990 Embassy Duty in Helsinki Finland.
This was taken at the Marine Corps Ball.

1990, Embassy Duty in Helsinki Finland. Here I am in
the reception line at the Marine Corps Ball

During the Bush Gorbachev Summit in Helsinki Finland in Sep 1990.
I was on Embassy Duty. Here is our Marine Detachment in Helsinki at
the American Embassy getting our picture with George H. Bush.

Photo taken in 1993 after I
came out for an article in the
New York Times. Taken by
Randy Davey.

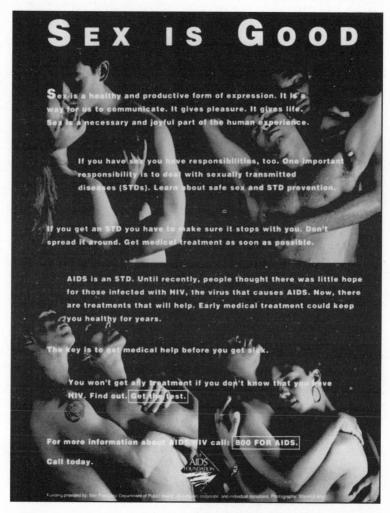

This ad, entitled "Sex Is Good", was used to kick-off AIDS Awareness Month for the San Francisco AIDS Foundation in 1992. The Marine Corps got upset at the time and tried to force them to take the ad down because one of the guys had a Marine Corps tattoo. Photo courtesy of San Francisco AIDS Foundation

This was taken in NYC during Gay Games IV. This is John and I after
he won his silver medal in Martial Arts

When I saw these bumper stickers, I knew I had to take a picture of these for history's sake

1996, Camp Lejeune, 2nd Supply BN, 2nd FSSG, working outside the warehouse. This is after I had come out and had been put back on active duty.

1996 Camp Lejeune, 2nd Supply BN, 2nd FSSG, working in Supply. This is after I had come out and had been put back on active duty.

1996, Field exercise, in Camp Lejeune having some fun. This is after I had come out and had been put back on active duty. There are openly gay servicemembers on duty in the field in the Marine Corps.

John and I in 1994 together at a fundraising event for an AIDS Charity. We were still in the Marine Corps at this time.

1995, this is on the USS Nassau. This is after I had come out and had been put back on active duty. Went on a little exercise up and down the east coast to Boston and Nova Scotia out of Norfolk, VA. This picture is taken in our bunk area of the ship. There are openly gay servicemembers on duty on ships in the Navy and Marine Corps.

CHAPTER 15
DISCHARGE

1100 hours 25 May 1993 Camp Lejeune, North Carolina

The day I got my semi-annual fitness report from Chief Warrant Officer Johnson, I already knew what was coming. Johnson had testified at my Discharge Board that he would rate me as "average" to / "above average." When I went into see him to get my fitness report and talk about it, as always he seemed uncomfortable. When I looked at the report I noticed that he had rated me as "above average" or "excellent" in most areas. No "outstandings" even though all my prior fitness reports from other supervisors had been. Any marks on the report dealing with how well I did the job, which he had said was a problem in my discharge hearing due to my legal problems, (attention to duty, economy of management, handling enlisted personnel and training personnel) were rated "above average" or "excellent." Judgment and loyalty, which are all-around measurements of my work were rated "average." This told the story that it wasn't really a job issue so much (legal problems taking me from work) as it was more an issue of what I had done, coming out, that bothered him. I asked him why he rated me as only "average" on judgment and loyalty. He said that he felt that I did not use proper judgment in what I did, referring to my stating that I am gay. He also questioned my loyalty to the Marine Corps for the same reason. He provided no other reason for the relatively low marks in these two areas. I believed that his evaluation of me was entirely based upon his disapproval of what I had done and my continued statements in the press.

His evaluation also failed to account for the disruptive effect of the Marine Corps anti-gay ban. I would not have been going to legal so much if the Marine Corps were not trying to discharge me. The Marine Corps was hurting itself. I specifically asked him why he rated me only "above average" in growth potential. He said, that in writing this fitness report he did not believe that you can be an activist and a Marine, and that the two do not mix. He failed to acknowledge that whatever activism I did on the side was on my own off-time outside of work hours when I was off base. In the end I walked out of his office seething. His own personal bias clouded his "judgment." Later I wrote a rebuttal to this fitness report and had it entered into my Service Record.

I could see that the discharge board was only the start and that they would continue every way to try to push me out. By not having any "outstanding" marks on the report and a couple of "average" marks, it was in effect a career-killer and I would never get promoted. He knew that. In keeping with the twisted logic, Major Ribadeneira reviewed the fitness report and stated that having to go to legal away from my work was caused by my own actions. Meaning it was my fault that the Marine Corps was kicking me out. I was wrong to stand up and say I was gay and therefore brought this on myself and the Marine Corps trying to kick me out was my own fault. Obviously the simple logic that if they had left me alone I would not have had to go to legal away from work escaped them.

In early June, word started leaking out in the press that there was a compromise coming down on the issue of whether to lift the ban. It was called, "Don't Ask, Don't Tell." When I was asked about it in the press I said, "The ban would still be basically in place. The compromise is not going to work. The new rule if approved would still discriminate against gays. It still forces gays and lesbians to lie."

Around the first of June an article came out in Details magazine, written by John Weir, about Jacksonville, North Carolina.

It was titled, "The Boys and the Ban - In the armed services fear among gay soldiers is running high. John Weir visits Camp Lejeune to uncover the roots of rage and self-loathing in the U.S. military." Weir had come down a couple of months prior from New York City and had spent some time in Jacksonville, North Carolina and Camp Lejeune, meeting and interviewing different people to get a good view of the town, its people, the Marine corps and its gay subculture with its dichotomy of straight, gay, and bisexual Marines, and their exploits off base. All the reporters from outside Jacksonville up to now had only been doing stories on the gays in the military issue from pretty much a political point of view but not really focusing on the town, its people, the culture of the area and the gay subculture within the military. In his article his descriptions of Jacksonville, North Carolina echo some of those of what Eric Schmitt briefly wrote about in the *New York Times* on the public forum, of a very religious, conservative, southern military town. John's story to some people was not very flattering of Jacksonville, as it sounded like a backward southern town right out of a movie, but the sad fact was his perception of the town was true to a "T."

His expose was well-written. He wrote about the local talk radio station and the local zealots who call in to the talk shows, a local social group with a membership of gays in and out of the military and how he was "contemplating the paradox of a closeted gay rights movement in such a town." He also mentions some of the scum that had come to Jacksonville from around the country to make a name for themselves over the gays in the military hoopla. One person in particular was a lawyer from Pittsburgh who started his own organization, where he was the only member, called "Straight Americans Military." He, along with a couple of other locals liked spreading lies and misinformation about gays and lesbians and got quite of bit press fanning the flames of hatred and bigotry throughout the town and base. While John Weir was

172

in town he and I ran around for a couple of days and I was straight up with him about what it was like living in this area and what John, my boyfriend, and I were going through as Marines and lovers. I explained how John had been harassed and how by me coming out I lost a few friends and the ones that I still had, I had to stay away from to protect them and their careers.

Weir talked to a few gay Marines and one in particular told him a story about how after that civilian, Crae Pridgen, was beaten up by those Marines in Wilmington, North Carolina outside Mikey Ratz, a gay bar, on January 29, the Marines in his office cheered and said, "finally somebody's doing something." The gay Marines who talked to John also told him how, since Clinton had announced getting rid of the ban on gays it was now harder on them now because all Marines were looking closer at people around them wondering who was gay and who was not, making everyone a bit more paranoid of being caught or seen as gay. Weir and I talked about the gay subculture in the Marines and he visited Friends Lounge and saw the unique relationship between Drag Queens and Marines. I told him a common joke in the gay military community from coast to coast, and I was later shocked that he printed it, but it was the truth none-the-less. "What's the difference between a straight Marine and a gay Marine? ... A six pack of beer."

I was explaining to John the hypocrisy of the Marine Corps going after gays in the Marines when there were so many Marines who fooled around. Some would call it situational sex, like what happened during Desert Storm, but other gay Marines and sailors would say it is much more than situational sex. Some of the gay Marines and sailors that he talked to agreed that if you took all the men as a whole in the Marines and split them out by what their sexual orientation was, that at least a third are either bisexual or gay.

John also heard from the gay Marines how the Marine Corps

is really like a quasi-religious order often compared to the Samurai and how the book of choice for Marines listed on the Marine Commandants reading list is the "Art of War" by Sun Tzu. Marines are trained to take care of their fellow Marines, like a brotherhood. It's an environment that promotes homoerotic bonding. Some would say the Marine Corps as an organization is the most homophobic of all the services but at the same time has the highest population of gays in it ranks out of all the services. It is an oxymoron. John of course found this out when he found it hard to find any "straight" Marines comfortable enough to talk to him about the issue of gays in the military. Of course, Weir ends the story with his own Friends Lounge experience on a Saturday night, watching the Drag Show and a bar full of Marines and sailors. The Drag Queen "Secret" is doing her pole dance and Drag Queen "Donna Saye" is performing "Lucy In The Sky With Diamonds." John meets a Marine at the bar who asks him to dance but yet the Marine insists he's not gay. John of course goes home with the guy and makes love. At the end of the day John has experienced what so many of us have known, if you want to meet a "straight" Marine.

In July it had been three months since my discharge board hearing and things were going better at work, as Chief Warrant Officer Johnson had left and I got a new Warrant Officer for a boss. I wasn't having to go to legal every couple of days and I was getting along well with the other Sergeants and troops in the unit. There was no "lack of unit cohesion" and actually some of the Marines and I joked about it in the office and most were like "What's the big deal?" when it came to my situation.

On Monday, July 19, President Clinton, the Commander in Chief of the Armed Forces finally announced the new policy. Clinton said it was "a major step forward." Nothing could have been further from the truth. A slick politician had sold us down the river. Down the drain, actually. It wasn't good. As head of the military he blinked and let the military rule the roost. Instead of getting out in front of this in 1992 as soon as he won the Presidency and calling in General Powell and the other Generals and treating this like Truman did when integrating African Americans into the military, he let it simmer and didn't have a strategy. This allowed the military to gain a foothold on the issue and generate congressional support against lifting the ban. President Clinton let General Powell and the military tell him what to do. Those of us who came out to make a difference got thrown under the bus. Since the new policy didn't allow a person to be out in the military that meant that the military would now move to discharge us. Lieutenant Zoe Dunning, who was one of those who came out, said, "The people who came out have been left to slide through the cracks. I'm disappointed he didn't stand his ground and do the right thing." Another person who had come out, Lieutenant Tracy Thorne said, "A lot of people say that we have taken a small step forward. We have not. The President and the Department of Defense have taken a fifty-year old policy, shined it up and added a few new words to it and called it progress. It's discrimination pure and simple. The President ran on a theme of change and hope. We haven't seen any change in the policy. What does the president stand for in this country?"

Petty Officer Keith Meinhold, another one who had come out said, he felt "betrayed" and that, "The battle is not over." Tanya Domi, a former Army Captain who worked for the National Gay and Lesbian Task Force, thought that Clinton had deferred to military leaders rather than seizing the issue as Commander in Chief. She said, "The president and Defense Chief, Les Aspin allowed the Joint Chiefs to engage in political logrolling." When I was asked by the press what I thought of it I said, "The policy is still very discriminatory and treats gays and lesbians as second class citizens." I pointed out the ambiguous guidelines about what constitutes homosexual conduct. I said, "something as simple as having a picture of a same sex friend or a copy of a gay news magazine could be interpreted as homosexual conduct. Some people might want to pursue that." I went on to say, "It's still going to cause gays and lesbians to look over their shoulder and lie."

One of the things that kept me going through this time was my attorneys. Lanny, Christopher, and Allan were amazing and kept telling me not to worry, we would continue to fight. It was great having these three guys in my corner.

On Thursday, July 22, Colonel Kahl, the Battalion Commanding Officer called me to his office for a chat. He said he was retiring the next week and that he wanted to clear up some lose ends. This seemed very strange in that I hadn't talked to him since before my discharge board in March. During the meeting he talked about his feelings on the president's decision and said that he felt the president had let the gay community down and that possibly the gay community had pushed this issue to early and too soon.

Like some other people that I had talked to since my discharge board, he tried to down play what my coming out had accomplished. He asked me what I thought I had accomplished. I told him and he said if only I had just kept quiet then I would have gotten my VSI/SSB benefits. At this point I realized he still didn't understand why I had come out even though I had told him before. In the long run, making a difference in the world was more important to me than getting my retirement money. In talking with him about the new policy I mentioned that Marines could now go to gay bars and associate with gays with no retributions. This was in reference to our February 5, meeting where he said "that they have a whole list of people that they believe are gay or lesbian." He said "we will still keep track of people and reports of people who associate with known gays and lesbians or go to gay bars." I was shocked that he was so arrogant and upfront about this Gestapo type of tactic. He felt that being gay and being a Marine were still considered wrong. The last thing he said to me was that I had a hard road ahead and he said that he didn't think I could meet the challenges, but of course I assured him I would and he said good luck and that was the end of the conversation.

Nothing else happened in July and as August rolled around an interesting story came to light in the press. On August 25, a controversy hit the papers out on the west coast. A porn king in California had been taking photos and producing gay porn videos of Marines. Some 200 to 500 Marines were said to have participated in these videos. This really didn't surprise me as there had been a similar controversy back in 1988. I was never asked about this in the press and it was definitely something that none of the straight Marines I knew talked about even though it was in all the papers. Even the Navy Times did a huge story on it. Something like this was very uncomfortable for anyone to talk about. It didn't last long in the press as it was something that the Marine Corps did not want to talk about.

On Friday afternoon, August 27, I was called up to the Battalion to see Personnel Officer, Warrant Officer Burg. I asked her what was going on and she said that they received a call from the liaison with Headquarter Marine Corps (HQMC) and the Justice Department and they were supposed to discharge me immediately. But she told them that they had to get me checked out first. She said that two messages had already been received but they did not contain the necessary instructions to discharge me. By Wednesday, September 1, they would, and she instructed me to start the process of turning in my military gear and checking out of my unit.

With a pretentious attitude, she told me that I should have just kept my mouth shut and I would have gotten my VSI/SSB, and now was getting nothing. As she handed me my checkout sheet, she said, "hurry up and checkout" and I said, "we will see." The problem was it was Friday afternoon and the whole base was already shutting down as "Emily," a category 3 hurricane was heading for the coast and was supposed to hit by Wednesday. I had no time to check out of all the places I needed to on base before being discharged. Warrant Officer Burg looked at me with disdain and said, snidely, "No, you will be gone by Wednesday."

I walked out of her office and got a copy of the Communication Message from HQMC. As I was read the message I noticed that a document review stamp was on it and several officers in the Battalion had already read and signed it. Officers like the Adjutant and Personnel Officer. Warrant Officer Templeman, who worked in Battalion Legal had also signed it and put a "smiley face" next to his signature. They were all in glee that I was going to be finally gone. I went back to my unit and talked to Warrant Officer Szatko and Major Ribidenria, both of whom expressed genuine disappointment that the Marine Corps was discharging me. Things had been going well in the office since everything had died down. That afternoon I was on the phone with Lanny, Christopher, and Allan and they assured me not to worry that they would be working to fight this.

Since John and I lived in a trailer house off base we spent Saturday boxing up some valuables, preparing for the incoming Hurricane and moving them over to our friends who had a house off base. They were a couple of Navy Corpsman that were together as a couple and they lived near us. All during the weekend I was really starting to worry about what I was going to do after I was discharged. John was still in the Marine Corps and I really didn't want to stay in Jacksonville, North Carolina and work there, as I really felt a lot of negativity about the backward city and all the hate that I got from the population. Jacksonville, North Carolina was primarily a service economy and, while it was honest work, it would have been way below my pay grade to go to work at Jiffy Lube or McDonald's, even if they would have hired me. I would have felt totally defeated. I couldn't sleep at all that weekend and had headaches.

On Monday, I started checking out and had a couple of interesting encounters. One of the requirements was that I go to a Transition Assistance Program (TAP) class which is mandatory for all Marines separating out of the Marine Corps. When I walked into the classroom there were some Marines already seated in the classroom. As soon as I took a seat, one Marine who was sitting next to me looked over and noticed who I was and immediately got his stuff and moved to a different seat. During the break there was an African American Marine who saw what had happened and came over and shook my hand to tell me good luck and that he appreciated what I did. It was the one bright spot in my day.

In the process of checking out I was at one of the offices on base and was waiting to see the clerk and I looked up at the bulletin board and saw that they had the Commandant of the Marine Corps, General Mundy's Statement on Equal Opportunity posted up there. General Mundy was noted in the press for being homophobic and had been responsible for helping circulate an anti-gay video, "The Gay Agenda" around the Pentagon. I started reading the paper and thought about how hypocritical he was. In the Equal Opportunity Statement he says, "We pride ourselves in the belief that every person who earns the title of Marine is entitled to be judged on his or her individual merit as a Marine, rather than upon differences such as gender, color, religion, culture or economic background. All Marines deserve the opportunity to achieve their full potential." I thought to myself, "yeah, right that is unless you're gay."

On Wednesday morning, September1, I went up to Battalion to check in and let them know what my progress was in checking out since today was supposed to be my last day. I got to see the message from HQMC. It said that they were to release me to the Standby Reserve on inactive status until October 1, 1993. In the Remarks Block of my DD- 214 (discharge form), it said to put final Discharge suspended until policy on homosexuals in the military announced July 19, 1993 becomes effective. Meaning even though

179

Clinton had announced the new policy in July the Pentagon was still writing the regulations and hadn't released them yet. When I saw Warrant Officer Burg, she told me with a sneering attitude that it didn't matter if I hadn't finished by the end of the day. She said, "you're going to be gone today," and then she curtly turned around and walked off.

I had to check in with Warrant Officer Templeman, the Battalion Legal Officer, and he had joy written all over his face when I talked to him. They at the Battalion were making a point of treating me with disdain and disgust the last day, as they were all celebrating my discharge. As I sat down at the admin clerk's desk to finish up some paperwork, he asked me for my military ID card. As I opened my wallet and pulled out my ID card and handed it to him. I felt suddenly like I was losing a part of myself, like they were asking me for my first born. He took my ID card and opened the drawer of his desk and pulled out a pair of huge scissors. As I watched, he cut up my ID card, right in front of me. At that moment I so wanted to order him to stop but I couldn't. My eyes filled with tears and a lump swelled up on my throat and I saw eleven wonderful years pass right before my eyes and I realized a part of me was now gone. I had played by the Marine Corps rules and had earned the title of Marine but now it was like all that I had worked for never mattered in their eyes.

After checking out at Battalion I slowly walked out of the building, contemplating what had just happened to me. I was in shock. I then went by my unit to say good-bye and get my one last fitness report from my supervisor.

I walked in and sat down and Warrant Officer Szatko gave me my fitness report and proceeded to talk about it to me. He said that "the problem with a situation such as yourself, it is like a dot on a piece of paper and it is a problem, everyone wants to move away from it." Warrant Officer Szatko had rated me as "Excellent to Outstanding" in all areas on my Fitness Report, like all the prior ones had been in my career until Chief Warrant Officer Johnson's report. His remarks on the report said:

"Intelligent, industrious, and articulate, MRO is aggressive and meticulous in completion of all duties. Capable, competent, and well versed in the mechanics of his duties. Duties include, researching, ordering, filing, and accounting for all Base Food Service Property purchases. During this reporting period MRO has ordered over 100,000 of food service equipment. Numerous vendors were contacted, long hours were required to research and order all equipment, MRO did, and directly supervised all stages of the process. Presents ideas in easily understood manner and written material requires virtually no editing. With present policy, MRO has limited growth potential. Recommend for promotion, based on overall performance."

Warrant Officer Szatko had rated me as "above average" in growth potential only because of the policy, because at the same time he recommended me for promotion. Major Ribadeneira's comments on the report were:

"Sergeant Elzie is an astute planner and organizer; a knowledgeable Marine who is technically proficient in the Supply field and has performed his duties in an outstanding manner. However Sergeant Elzie's professed homosexual preferences and current Department of Defense, (DOD) policy preclude recommending his promotion."

So this would be the first time since coming out that I would be recommended for promotion. However due to the policy the higher ups would say "no can do."

After meeting with Warrant Officer Szatko I gathered my things and drove off base to go home.

I got to the trailer house and as I walked in the door I sat down on the couch. I felt like it was all over and I felt like shit. John came home and tried to cheer me up and that night we went out and ate and spent some quality time together. Thank God John was there to be my rock because I don't know what would have happened if he hadn't. It was then I realized I was the first Marine and the first servicemember to be discharged under "Don't Ask, Don't Tell."

CHAPTER 16
REINSTATEMENT

0900 hours 7 September 1993 Camp Lejeune, North Carolina

On September 7, I left for Washington D.C. to meet with my attorneys. After my discharge, Covington & Burling decided to file suit in U. S. Federal District Court in Washington, D.C. to get me reinstated. I went up to D.C. for a press conference on September 8, with my attorneys, Lanny Breuer, Christopher Sipes and Allan Moore as they had filed a suit on my behalf. Here was my statement for the press conference:

"It is with courage and determination that I am before you today to announce that we have filed suit against the Secretary of Defense, the Secretary of the Navy, and the Commandant of the Marine Corps, for discharging me from the Marines just because I am gay."

"Today is only the beginning and to borrow a popular phrase, "we've only just begun" in this rightful cause. I personally will not rest until I see this discriminatory policy lifted so that no more dedicated American Service members lives are ruined by this unjust policy."

"Seven months ago I stepped into this fight to effect a positive change and to help my fellow gay brothers and sisters in the military. As an upright American who believes in the ideals of liberty and justice for all, and that all people are created equal, I could not and will not stay silent."

"The American military has been pulling the wool over the American public's eyes about the discrimination going on in the

U.S. Military." "The bottom line is this, that the military's discriminatory policy on gays and lesbians has no basis, and I repeat, no basis, in fact. As we all know, study after study has been done, all supporting the lifting of the ban and the facts are in our corner consistently. The truth will come out, and that is that the current policy discriminates not on the basis of the performance of service members like myself but on misguided stereotypes. To put it quite simply it is based on prejudice."

"We have even heard some people say that some discrimination is okay. Well, I don't know what country they were raised in, but I was raised in this great country of ours and I have helped defend it and I have faith that most Americans disdain any form of discrimination and will see the truth about this policy. I am confident that truth will win out and we will win. Thank you."

After this news conference it was just a waiting game to see what the courts would do next. And I went back to North Carolina to figure out what I was going to do next.

When I got back John and I both resigned from the North Carolina Veterans Coalition because we just had too much going on in our lives at that point and had to take care of ourselves and try to figure out what our next steps would be. John was still in the Marines and his enlistment wasn't up until October 1995, and I had to find a job. Meanwhile, in Washington, Lanny, Chris and Allan were working hard to get me back on active duty. On September 16 they wrote an excellent op-ed in The Washington Times, titled, "The New Old Policy on Gays in Uniform." It talked about the illogical rationale for "Don't Ask, Don't Tell," and how that related to my case.

When I got back to North Carolina from D.C., I got a call from a producer at MTV who wanted me to participate in a show that they were going to do in October, called "Free Your Mind." I decided to participate and on October 10 I took off for New York City to be on the show. "Free Your Mind" highlighted your people discussing popular issues of the day. The topic for the show that I was going to be filmed doing was on gay and lesbian issues. It included about twenty people (gay, lesbian, bisexual and straight) and we all sat on the stage discussing the issue. What I didn't realize was that the producer had also called the Marine Corps and invited a straight Marine to give his point of view.

This to me was just frustrating that people didn't see this as an ethical and moral issue. To me, the ban on gays in the military was a crime against humanity. How could people debate a person's equal rights? How could someone debate whether to ruin someone's life and treat them as a second class citizen? I knew that I would have my work cut out on the show. When I got there I met the Marine, who, as it happened, worked for Major Farrar in the Public Affairs office in Camp Lejeune. We had some interesting discussions on the side about gays in the military, and while he agreed they were in the Marines and did a good job, he admitted he was uncomfortable with living with gay men.

He surprised me by mentioning the rumor that former Commandant of the Marine Corps, General Gray, was gay. I had heard this rumor over and over again in the past two or three years. General Gray was someone who I continued to look up to as an outstanding Marine. During the taping of the show he of course agreed that gays and lesbians perform just as well as straight Marines, and that there were Marines he knew besides me who were gay, and that gays and lesbians were in the foxholes and showers, but still, he said he personally would be uncomfortable with living with gay men. I of course pointed out that I had been in foxholes and showered with Marines who knew I was gay, and there had been no problems. Someone else on the show also pointed out that in fire departments and police departments, straight men and gay men shower together and nothing happens.

Another guy on the show pointed out that straight men also check out other men in the showers if not to just compare. At that remark there were laughs, and tension and they took a commercial break in the show, but it was a well-made point and one that I knew a lot of straight Marines would be uncomfortable admitting to it, even though it happens. I don't know if I helped some young person's life watching the show that day, but I hope I did.

After the taping of the show I took off to visit some friends up in Vermont. I needed a break from all that had happened so I could figure out what I was going to do next in my life. I couldn't depend that the judge would put me back on active duty, so my friends Gene Barfield, and his husband, Tim LaCroix invited me to come stay with them in Vermont for a couple of weeks, to relax and get my head cleared. I had been experiencing stress-related symptoms the entire past year, having headaches and not sleeping well, and I needed a break.

One morning, about a week into my getaway at Gene and Tim's, I was at the breakfast table drinking coffee when I got a call from Lanny. He had Chris and Allan in his office and he asked me if I wanted him to give me the good news first of the bad news first. I was on the edge of my seat and I expected the worst. I said, "the good news first." Lanny then told me that due to the U.S. District Court Judge Hatter's decision in the Meinhold case, the Marine Corps was putting me back on active duty effective immediately and I was to report back to my former command. Judge Stanley Sporkin, who was the judge in my case in U.S. District Court in D.C., was still looking at my case for declaratory and injunctive relief. I asked Lanny what the bad news was, and he, Chris and Allan laughed and said my vacation was over. At that moment my spirits could not have been higher. Not since the day that I had come out were my spirits higher. After profusely thanking my attorneys, I got off the phone and told Gene, who couldn't have been happier for me. I called the house and left a message for John and I immediately made plans to catch the next bus south back to North Carolina.

When the press got wind that I was being put back on active duty October 20, they began interviewing my attorneys, the Marine Corps and me. The Marine Corps was downplaying it and figured that I would be out again soon. One thing that I found interesting was the sudden honesty by one of the Marine Corps Public Affairs officer's remarks to the press. Major Mark Huges said: "Elzie's short reinstatement had not had a bad effect on the base. The Marines didn't make a big deal about it because it wasn't a big deal. He was treated like any other Marine coming back from reserve duty. He's acting like the professional soldier that he is." I thought, "Wow!" Here they were in a way finally admitting that an openly gay Marine wasn't causing any bad morale or unit cohesion problems for the Marines on base. When the press asked me how I felt I said, "I am thrilled, I am so happy right now you would not believe it. I am really happy to be going back to work. My main goal is to go back to work and do a good job and take it one day at a time."

When I checked back into the battalion on Wednesday October 20, I made a point of sticking my head into Warrant Officer Burg's office and saying "Good Morning, Mam." She had nothing to say. There were some people who were not happy, that I was back, but as a general rule everyone I dealt with was professional and there were no negative comments. I found out as I was checking in that I wouldn't be going back to the Marine Corps Base Food Service Office to work. I would be working in the same building, but now I would be working at Marine Corps Base Logistics Office.

On November 1, Judge Stanley Sporkin issued a temporary restraining order telling the Marine Corps that they couldn't kick me out. He at one point described the government's conduct in the case as "so un-American, it's unbelievable." Judge Sporkin said that his order would remain in effect for ten days, during which time he planned to prepare a written decision on my request for a longer lasting injunction. After this I was quoted in the press saying, "I want to remain on active duty, hoping to prove a point that gays can serve in the military without affecting the job performance of colleagues. We are just continuing to stress that point. There hasn't been any lack of unit cohesion or anything like that." I pointed out that: "I served for eight months, openly gay with no problems, and I've been back since the 20th with again no incidents or negative problems or anything like this." I explained that my case proves that openly gay people can serve in the military. "What we're looking at is the argument that openly gay service members cause bad morale is a tired argument." I also said, "I missed the job, the camaraderie. I think the Marine Corps is a good organization. I love it. But it has to make some changes to get rid of some of the discrimination." Lanny was quoted in the press as saying, "Everyone realizes if everyone stops playing politics, gays, heterosexuals will just do their jobs. The ban makes no sense. Our country is not permitted to make laws based on irrational fear and prejudice."

Then, on November 11, Judge Stanley Sporkin issued a thirteen-page opinion. He ruled that I could remain in the Marine Corps until my lawsuit was settled. In his thirteen-page opinion, Judge Sporkin indicated that the Marine Corps' actions against me likely violated both the equal protection guarantee of the Fifth Amendment and the free speech guarantee of the First Amendment. He stated that I had presented a strong case, and that I will probably succeed in establishing that the policy banning homosexuals from the military solely on the basis of status serves no legitimate governmental purpose. He chided the defendants for apparently wanting to punish me because of my statements that I was gay, and noted that I did not become any less of a Marine on the day I announced my sexual orientation. He noted that my service record was replete with commendations, awards, and decorations.

He wrote, "The ability of homosexuals to perform in all phases of the workplace, including the armed services has been proven beyond any question. There is simply no correlation between an individual's sexual orientation and his or her intellectual or physical capacity to perform in the workplace. Indeed, in considering the public interest, it might well be argued that to deprive our armed forces of the intellectual and physical prowess of some extraordinarily talented individuals strictly because of their sexual orientation would be doing a great disservice to this nation."

I was quoted in the press after his opinion was released saying, "I am extremely pleased that the Court appears to understand what has happened in my case, and I hope that this ruling, along with other positive rulings, will lead to the ending of discrimination in the military against gays and lesbians."

On October 31, Commandant of the Marine Corps, General Carl Mundy, put his foot in his mouth and made some racist statements about minority officers in the Marine Corps on the CBS News Program "60 Minutes." He said: "In the military skills, we find that the minority officers do not shoot as well as the non-minorities. They don't swim as well. And when you give them a compass and send them across the terrain at night in a land navigation exercise, they don't do as well at that sort of thing." He was forced to issue an apology afterwards. Two weeks later, on November 10, for his annual "Commandant's Message to the Marine Corps" for the 218th Birthday of the Marine Corps he addressed the subject. In his message he made a commitment to make the Marines reflect the "Fabric of the Nation." I really wish that I could have asked him in public, in front of a camera about that statement, because I would have pointed out to him that gays and lesbians are an integral part of that "Fabric of the Nation" that he talked about. Why couldn't he accept gays and lesbians in the Marines?

As soon as I got reinstated back to active duty, John and I realized that we were going to have to move back onto base in our respective Barracks. Me with my unit, Marine Corps Base, Headquarters Battalion, and he out at the Marine Corps Base, Rifle Range. The year had taken a huge toll on both of our expenses with the traveling that I had to do back and forth to D.C. So in November, we moved back into the barracks as we couldn't afford living off base anymore. In December, John came over to my barracks room one night and we had a heart-to-heart talk. We had both changed over the past ten months. Our relationship, too, was changing, and because we were in separate units we didn't live together anymore. I felt I needed a break. I wanted us to spend some time away from each other but he didn't. I felt I needed space, yet John felt hurt that I wanted to break up. I felt guilty because he really had stuck by me in so many ways and I was hurting him by wanting to break up.

My coming out in January had irreparably damaged our relationship. He had come to grips with me coming out and affecting his career in the Marines, but down deep inside he didn't think I cared for him, because of what I had done. Yet he still stuck by me over those ten months and loved me. He felt I chose coming out, over his career and his feelings. The fact was, I did, and was guilty of that. Standing in my barracks room that night he asked me what was it going to be? Were we going to go our separate ways or were we going to stay together? At that moment I couldn't bring myself to hurt him because I truly loved him. More like a brother than a lover. I said that we were going to stay together. But when he left I felt guilty and had to ask myself was I using him? Was I so scared of losing the one person who stuck by me the whole time that I was willing to stay with him even though my love for him was different than his love for me? As he walked out the door of my room back to his barracks, I really didn't think our relationship was going to last.

CHAPTER 17
PROVING MYSELF ONCE MORE

0900 hours 8 January 1994 Camp Lejeune, North Carolina

Living in the barracks now was pretty lonely because I didn't live with John. I had a barracks room to myself. Some Sergeants in my unit had their own rooms and others had roommates. I think the barracks office was making sure they didn't give me a roommate to make a point. Saturday morning as I waited for John to come over to my barracks room, I started making out a list of what I needed to get at the store that day when he got over here. As we got into the new year, John and I really tried to look ahead with a positive attitude and spend more time togethI felt like I had finally arrived at a unique point in my life in the Marines, where I was now doing what I had always wanted to do and that was to serve openly. I didn't have to worry about who knew I was gay and the stress of hiding that. This was so different than what all of my other gay Marine friends were going through. They had the stress of being in the closet and having to constantly look over their shoulders. I really felt like I had crossed a bridge or divide but all of my gay military friends were still left on the other side of that divide and it was like we lived in two different worlds and we couldn't necessarily relate anymore. For example, surprisingly after coming out, it didn't feel comfortable for me to continue to use the code word "family" to refer to gay men and lesbians anymore because it was like going back into the closet. I felt like I was growing and moving on in my life in different ways and they were being held back. For me it was a liberating, but lonely experience. I, however, did have the stress of everyone watching me and while there were many people supporting me, there were just as many who wanted me to screw up.

I knew I was going to be in the Marines for a while, and I wanted to see how far I could go in breaking that glass ceiling for a gay Marine. Could I get promoted? Probably not, even though since coming out I had been recommended for promotion. There would be people high up in the Marines who would not let that happen. The most I could hope for was to continue to do a good job, be an example, and pursue possibly going on a field exercise on a ship so that I could point out that the arguments against openly serving gays on ships and in the foxholes was an ignorant point of view. The way I saw it, someone's bigoted discomfort shouldn't keep me from serving my country and being successful doing that. It really was all about from here on out just settling down, doing my job and getting on with my career in the Marines. But unbeknownst to me this wouldn't be a quiet or easy year.

Things were going well at my new unit. The troops and fellow NCO's were comfortable around me. I had a cubicle at work and like the other Marines I had pictures on the corkboard in my cube. For eleven years I had always wanted to put up a picture of my boyfriend at work like the other guys put up their girlfriends and wives. So I put up a picture of John, since people in my unit didn't know him, and a picture of me with former President Bush while I was on Embassy Duty.

John was in the process of putting in the paperwork to compete in Martial Arts (Karate) at Gay Games IV in New York City in June. He had been a Karate State Champ in Massachusetts while in high school before he came into the Marine Corps. We were planning on taking a couple of weeks leave in June while in New York City during the Gay Games. Because we were now living in the barracks we got away on the weekends to get off base. We had a few friends down in Wilmington, North Carolina associated with

St. Jude's Metropolitan Community Church, so we spent some time down there on the weekends.

Even as the Marine Corps and some Marines were trying to make my life hell, it never surprised me the support I would get from some of the most unlikely places. There was a friend of mine in Raleigh, North Carolina who had a friend who was a North Carolina State Trooper, former Marine, and gay. This North Carolina State Trooper and my other friend knew several gay police officers around the nation and they decided to contact a few of them in an effort to obtain a shoulder patch from each of them with the understanding they would be sent to me as a show of support. Well, when it was all said and done they sent me patches from all over the country. I got patches from: the New York City Police Department, New York State Police, Virginia State Police, Boston Police Department, Florida Highway Patrol, Atlanta Police Department, Chicago Police Department, Honolulu Police Department, California Highway Patrol and many others. It was one of the most amazing things that ever happened to me and definitely helped me through some of the tough times knowing there were gay police officers and highway patrolmen out there pulling for me.

In March, John met another Marine in his Rifle Range unit who was gay. His name was Maylan Thomas. I think it was a good thing for both of them to have a kindred spirit in the same unit. I was glad so that John wouldn't feel so alone out at the Rifle Range.

Shortly thereafter, I went out on a field exercise for a week where I was a Squad Leader in charge of eight Marines out there. We had to set up some defensive positions and had several foxholes on our perimeter. It was a lot of fun and I got along with all the Marines well. During the exercise I had to share a two-man foxhole and tent with another Marine. At the time I wondered what General Mundy would have thought of a gay Marine out in the field with his squad of Marines and in the foxholes and nothing happening. Also that month, I was awarded another Good Conduct Medal. This was the twisted logic of my situation. Since I had come out, I was an openly gay Marine in the foxholes with other Marines with no problems, I had outstanding fitness reports, I was recommended for promotion, I was awarded a Good Conduct Medal, and yet the Marine Corps was trying to discharge me.

Since I had moved back into the barracks and was spending more time on base, I started noticing certain things that I hadn't noticed before. There were some vehicles on base that had anti-gay bumper stickers on them. One said, "Take a Stand, Keep the Ban" another one said, "Not in my Corps" and had a circle over the word Gays. One day at one of my friend's barracks I was walking past one of the barracks rooms and I noticed that there was a sign in the barracks room window that said, "Support your local gay basher in the Marine Corps." When I mentioned this to some of the other gay Marines I knew, they said that they had seen several of these signs in Marine's barracks windows around the base. The sad fact was that the military leadership allowed this. I thought it was unethical and criminal and didn't reflect what Marines were supposed to stand for. Because it wasn't my barracks or my unit I really couldn't say anything. If the First Sergeant of that unit allowed that then there was no way a complaint by me not in that unit would have changed that. I thought it was shameful.

In April I got a fitness report from my new supervisor, Major Gray. He rated me as "outstanding" in all areas: Handling Enlisted Personnel, Training personnel, Personal Appearance, Military Presence, and Attention to Duty, Initiative, Judgment, Cooperation, Force, Economy of Management, Leadership, Loyalty, and Growth Potential. He rated me as "excellent" in Administrative duties. He also marked that I was qualified for promotion. He wrote,

"Sergeant Elzie is a personal NCO, amiable and likeable. Honest, sincere, with the highest integrity, he is meticulously thorough in his work. A rapid and intense worker, he produces accurate and timely results. He possesses a high degree of initiative and requires a minimum of supervision, and choice of methods of accomplishing desired results are exceptionally good. Likeable, with an excellent sense of humor, and an ingrained respect for his fellow Marine, he secures a high degree of loyalty and cooperation from his subordinates in whom he instills a great sense of personal responsibility for the quality of their work. His subordinates respect him and honor his judgment, as he is always willing to and does accept their suggestions when they have merit."

When my fitness report went up the chain to Major Gray's boss, Colonel Fletcher, he made comments on the report.

"I do not disagree with the Reporting Senior's evaluation of Sergeant Elzie's technical competence and his work ethic. Nor do I disagree that the results of Sergeant Elzie's efforts are not generally well above the norm, considering his time in grade and time in service and in this supporting establishment environment of Base Logistics. I have directly and indirectly observed these things myself. However, given his professed sexual preferences and Department of Defense policy regarding homosexual conduct, Sergeant Elzie cannot be considered qualified for retention. Thus, he cannot be considered qualified for promotion."

In looking at these Fitness Reports since I came out, it was clear that the Marine Corps was not going to let me move up the ladder even if my supervisors were recommending me for promotion. I was starting to see that the Marine Corps was slowly putting the screws to me and biding their time. So far, they had lost at trying to kick me out, so all they had to do was make sure I didn't get promoted, and I would never be able to stay in the Marine Corps long term even if I won in court.

You see, there is a requirement that a Marine has to pick up a certain rank by a certain amount of years, and if you don't get to that rank then you have to get out. If I wasn't promoted by a certain time in the Marines then I would have to get out, even if I won in court. Again, I was playing by the rules and trying to pursue staying in but it was going to be a battle of wills.

In early June, I got a surprise phone call from a Marine who was stationed in Charleston, S.C., Corporal Kevin Blaesing. He was going through a similar situation as I was. In confidence, he had told his doctor, "I think I might be gay," and the doctor told his Commanding Officer. His Commanding Officer, Lieutenant Colonel Ronald Rueger was not interested in pursuing the information and ignored the report. However, when he retired, Kevin's incoming Commanding Officer Lieutenant Colonel. M. J. Martinson pursued it and tried to pressure Kevin to quit, telling him that he brought shame to the Marine Corps.

Lieutenant Colonel M. J. Martinson told Kevin that he thought homosexuals were "disgusting." Thank God, Kevin had an attorney and Servicemembers Legal Defense Network, (SLDN) was helping him. Michelle Benecke and Dixon Osburn, who ran SLDN, were amazing, and what I would call guardian angels for a lot of gay servicemembers going through hard times with the military. Since I had already been through this for a year with the Marine Corps, I gave Kevin what advice I thought would help him. I listened to him and tried to be as supportive as possible, even though he was on another base in a different state. Kevin was an outstanding Marine who had excellent performance evaluations and was Marine of the Quarter for his unit. Now, however, his new Commanding Officer was going after him with a vengeance and was trying to downgrade his performance evaluations.

I was pissed off the Marine Corps was going after him, and it just made me all the more determined to continue to speak out about these issues. It felt like the Marine Corps was going after one of my own troops. I wished Kevin had been in my unit so I could have watched out for him since he was junior to me in rank. I really didn't like the Marine Corps treating gay and lesbian Marines like this. It was good for my spirits talking to him. I was finally talking to another Marine that understood what I was going through.

After I got off the phone with him I just knew deep down in my heart that the fight I was battling was worth it so that I could stop these types of abuses from happening to my fellow gay and lesbian Marines. Kevin and I would become good friends and a couple of months later he came up to visit John and I at Camp Lejeune.

On June 13, John and I left for New York City for Gay Games IV and Stonewall 25. The Gay Games is a huge international event that takes place every four years. Participants from over 70 countries compete in 34 sports disciplines. For the first time since 1992 when we first met, I was happy to be able to support John in something that was really important for him. On the second day of the Martial Arts competition, John won a Silver Medal. It was an amazing and happy time for both of us. It was great to see John competing in his element. I will never forget watching John walk out during the opening ceremonies and then the closing ceremonies, which were at Yankee Stadium. I was so proud of him. I think this time away from Lejeune really helped our relationship and helped get out some of the stress that we had been under for the past year and half. After the Gay Games, John and I drove back to North Carolina, stopping in Washington, D.C. for a couple of days to spend time with friends.

During this time, Michelle and Dixon with SLDN were tracking numerous abuses by the military under "Don't Ask, Don't Tell." The military was still asking, still investigating and still pursuing gays and lesbians with a vengeance, effectively ignoring the policy. For example, in July a gay Marine friend of mine out in San Diego, sent me a written policy order that had been sent out from the Staff Judge Advocates Office for the Marine Corps Recruit Depot and Western Recruiting Region for the Marines, which covers all recruiting stations in states west of the Mississippi river. It was the new Department of Defense, (DOD) policy on Homosexual Conduct and it talked about how "Don't Ask, Don't Tell" was supposed to be implemented. It had an extra signature page for signatures and comments from everyone in the command from the Assistant Chief of Staff, to the Operations Officer, (OPSO) for the Western Region. The Assistant Operations Officer put a long statement on the comments section stating his disagreement with the policy:

"OPSO, Recruiters should be able to screen or ask applicants about past homosexual conduct. This is analogous to drug screening where we ask what drugs were used, the amounts and how frequently, this allows us to judge the probability or propensity for the applicant's future drug use and whether he or she should be waived for enlistment. Similarly, for homosexual behavior such questions ought to be asked in order to judge propensity for future activity and whether or not such applicants should be waived for enlistment furthermore like our drug policy each applicant should be warned that homosexual conduct or propensity is not tolerated in the military and that such actions or tendencies could result in punitive or administrative discharge."

The fact is that having a leader questioning the policy just let all of the recruiters and drill instructors know in the western United States that it was still okay to question applicants and recruits and to defy the order. SLDN found numerous examples of these abuses. Besides SLDN being a support network, there were quite a few gay military personnel who were corresponding online as a support network for one another. There was an American Online, (AOL) Group, "Military City Online" and under that there was a gay military group. Zoe Dunning, Keith Meinhold, Tracey Thorne, Rich Richenberg, other active duty and gay veterans, and I, all kept in touch and shared information. There was also a network to funnel people in trouble to SLDN. While I was at Camp Lejeune, I referred a few Marines to SLDN for help when they were being investigated.

In September of 1994, I went to the Rifle Range for my yearly qualification. I ended up qualifying in the highest category which is Expert with a 237 out of a possible 250 points. I was the high shooter for my detail that week on the Rifle Range. Since I had been in the Marines, I found that I really liked being on the Rifle Range and shooting weapons. I was qualified as a Rifle Expert and a Pistol Expert. The Marine Corps prides itself on marksmanship skills and it is considered the most valued skill for a Marine to have. The importance of your rifle and being able to shoot well are drilled into you, because in combat it can mean the difference between life and death. In Marine Security Guard School I was named pistol high shooter for my class. At one time I was going to try out for the Marine Corps Rifle Competitions after getting back to the states off Embassy Duty but I just never had the time. John was also a very good marksman and did compete. When asked later by the press about my time at the Rifle Range after coming out, I just said that I used the Rifle Range to relax and I found a certain calmness and concentration in shooting a weapon. It helped me to de-stress. Later, in September, the Navy Times published a profile on me as an update of what was going on with "Don't Ask, Don't Tell" and how things were going for me in my second year of serving openly in the Marine Corps. They mentioned my high shooter score at the Rifle Range and mentioned my last fitness report from Major Gray where I had received "outstandings" and was recommended for promotion. They also mentioned Colonel Fletcher's rebuttal, that because of my "professed sexual preference" and DOD policy I could not be consider qualified for retention or promotion. This story created a huge firestorm, but was also a watershed event in how I was looked at in the Marine Corps by many Marines.

After this story ran, there was a deluge of responses in the national press, and correspondence to me. On base, my face-to-face interactions with other Marines were overwhelmingly positive. It was like I had broken through a ceiling and had found a new respect among the Marines I ran into. Attitudes changed from contempt to respect. At the same time, those in the Marine Corps who didn't want me in were livid. They went after me that much harder. There were a couple of Sergeants who wrote to the local paper saying that I had dishonored the Marine Corps by saying I was gay. It was clear that they had problems seeing that a gay Marine could be doing well in the Marines and it went against their own prejudices. The Marine Corps had tried to make an example out of me by dragging me through the mud and now anything that was positive that came out about me just flew right back in their face. As I dealt with Marines in the course of my job on base many would say to me that they didn't realize I was still in and that they saw the article, and told me to "hang in there."

One situation in particular surprised me. I was standing outside the chow hall a couple of days after the Navy Times article ran and this Hummvee pulls up and stops right in front of me. This big African American Staff Sergeant jumped out and came over to me, reached out his hand and thanked me for what I was doing. He, told me to "hang in there." I was surprised that he did this, and at the same time overwhelmed that I didn't know what to say back to him except, "thanks." I had noticed that consistently, since coming out when it came to support from other Marines, nine times out of ten they were usually African American or Hispanic. I think after the story ran, most people saw that it spoke to an issue of basic fairness and injustice. After all that the Marine Corps was putting me through, I was still out there doing a good job—so much so that Marine Corps Officers were bucking the system and recommending me for promotion, and the higher-ups were saying the only reason I could not be promoted was because I had said I was gay.

After Colonel Fletcher's rebuttal to Major Gray on my fitness report, I realized I needed a change of command. I didn't see myself going anywhere under Colonel Fletcher or any Marine Corps Base command because none of them were deployable. I wanted to get over to a deployable unit so that I could go on a ship and get out in the field more. So I put in a request to be transferred to the Second Marine Division or to the Second Force Service Support Group, (FSSG). I would have to wait and see if it would be approved, as Colonel Fletcher didn't want to see me go to another unit.

On October 27, I drove up to D.C. for the "Ending the Witch Hunts" Dinner, an SLDN benefit at the Tutorsky Mansion. I was on the Honorary Host Committee as was Lieutenant Dirk Selland and Lieutenant J.G. Tracy Thorne. All of us were servicemembers challenging the military policy on gays and lesbians. Featured guests were also servicemembers fighting the military policy on gays and lesbians: Colonel Margarethe Cammermeyer, Captain Rich Richenberg, and Corporal Kevin Blaesing. It was great to finally meet Kevin and to see Michelle and Dixon again, who were working hard to help people after Clinton's "Don't Ask, Don't Tell" policy was put in place.

Servicemembers Legal Defense Network was the only organization watching out for gay and lesbian servicemembers and tracking the issue. They would get calls from all over the world, night and day, from servicemembers still going through horrible interrogations and investigations. After the 1993 debate on gays in the military, gay organizations like the Human Rights Campaign Fund, (HRCF) moved on to other issues and dropped the issue of "Don't Ask, Don't Tell" (DADT) like a hot potato. Gay and Lesbian servicemembers had nowhere to turn for help. Michelle Benecke, a lawyer, and former Army Captain, and Dixon Osburn, a bright lawyer, both of whom had worked with the Campaign for Military Service, realized that something had to be done. As Michelle said, "We just finally said, somebody has to do something. These people were incredibly courageous and nobody out there was taking care of them. I guess in some ways, my work with SLDN is because I still feel responsible for my troops."

So they both decided to create a national organization. They could not get any money from any gay organization but they had a lot of letters of support from legal groups. With the help of gay servicemembers like Midshipmen Joseph Steffan, Lieutenant Zoe Dunning and Colonel Margarethe Cammermeyer, and volunteer help from Jeff Matchan, Ed Fox, and National Gay and Lesbian Task Force board member Ruth Eisenberg, they found space and raised money. They created a huge network of attorneys to be able to help servicemembers. By February, 1994, SLDN had responded to calls from over 400 servicemembers and the numbers were going up. To me and many others, Michelle and Dixon are heroes in the gay community.

One of the dynamics of the politics within the gay community is the gay lobbyists in D.C., and how some of them really felt about the "gays in the military" issue. There were some that didn't really think that we should have been fighting for gays to be able to serve in the military, and that there were more important issues and the ban on gays in the military had virtually no impact on the greater gay and lesbian community. I was rather incensed by this myopic view, especially after all I had been through. This view was something that I had experienced from a few people in the community since starting to work as an activist. In December, The Washington Blade, a gay newspaper in D.C., ran a letter to the editor that I had submitted in rebuttal to an opinion piece written by a D.C. gay lobbyist, Alexander Robinson. Here is my letter.

"Writing off the Military"

"In the October 26 Washington Blade, Alexander Robinson a lobbyist on Gay and AIDS issues for the American Civil Liberties Union, commented that "the codification of the ban on Gays and Lesbians in the military was huge loss," he went on to say:

"That said, I question how we assess that loss. What kind of loss was it? Yes, we did not want the ban to be codified but what impact will it have on the community and was the process worthwhile even?"

"He also mentioned that the military's treatment of gays, while having serious civil rights implications, has a limited direct impact on the majority of the community, since many gays oppose a large military presence and gays who serve in the military comprise a small segment of the community at large."

"As a current active duty United States Marine who came out publicly last year and did some lobbying in Washington with some of the lobbyists, I feel that Robinson's comments are just one example of why we have (temporarily) lost the battle of the ban."

"There are a total of 1.6 million personnel in the armed forces right now. This doesn't include reserves or National Guard units. Considering that the military is the single largest sector of government employment and using conservative estimates that one out of every ten people in the military is either Gay or Bisexual we could reasonably conceive that there is a large number of Gay and Bisexual personnel who are currently serving their country in silence."

"If the ban had been struck down the military would have been forced to institute gay diversity and sensitivity training, a lot like what large corporations are doing today, and as is currently done in the military with regard to required sexual harassment and racism awareness classes."

"Just think about it, 1.6 million people would have to have gone through a gay awareness class. Talk about mass education! Let's just suppose now what happens when those same people who went through that class and also had to work with somebody who is openly gay get out of the military and go back to their local communities."

"These people, because of their positive military experiences working with gay men and lesbians, might be more likely to support our community especially when fighting anti-gay initiatives."

"I feel Alexander Robinson's comments sadly show a lack of vision. He seems willing to write off the military issue now. He does not understand that the military ban does and continues to have a major direct impact on our community. Anytime that our government has a discriminatory policy that treats us as second class citizens, it affects all of us!"

"Contrary to what Robinson thinks, it was a worthwhile process. We came out, we grew, we learned and we educated a lot of people. But it's not over and we will continue to fight against the ban until we win. We will win! I just hope that Alexander Robinson and lobbyists like him will continue to help us fight against the military ban until that day."

Sergeant Justin Elzie United States Marine Corps.

At the end of November my request for a transfer was approved to go to a deployable unit. I got orders to Commanding General, Second FSSG, Second Supply Battalion, Camp Lejeune, North Carolina. I was supposed to report by no later than December 30. Because I would be leaving Marine Corps Base that meant I would get one last fitness report. I was still working in the same office with the same Marines, except Major Gray had since left in the eight months since my last report. So that meant Captain Reinhold would be evaluating me.

On December 12, I went in to see Captain Reinhold. I expected the same kind of report that I got from Major Gray since nothing had changed in the office in the eight months that had gone by since my last report. I reported to him and sat down. He reached across the desk and said with a grin on his face: "I'm sure this fitness report is not going to be as good as you expected."

I started to read the fitness report and at first my heart sank and then I started to get mad. On the fitness report I got no "outstandings" in any area and for the first time in my Marine Corps career I got "below averages." He rated me as below average in: handling enlisted personnel, and leadership. He rated me as average in loyalty and everything else on the report as "above average" or "excellent." His remarks were:

"Sergeant Elzie is tactful and courteous, possesses congenial personality. Due to professed homosexuality, loyalty shown him by juniors is questionable, working relationship with others suffers. Cooperative attitude but unable to get best effort from Marines with who he associates. Will have some difficulty serving at more senior levels. Bases on my estimate of this Marine's potential, I recommend that he not be promoted at anytime."

As soon as I read his comments on my fitness report, my first reaction was shock, and then my heart sank because I knew what they were trying to do to me and then I started getting mad. Considering the positive comments that I had received from Gunnery Sergeant Brown, Master Gunnery Sergeant Gully, and Gunnery Sergeant Baxter, all immediate supervisors, even Captain Reinhold himself since my last fitness report, this was outrageous.

What was glaring was that there was an obvious pattern here. The Marine Corps was trying to downgrade my fitness report, just as they had with Corporal Blaesing. What was also glaring was he didn't recommend me for promotion even though I had been recommended on both my last fitness reports since coming out. And on my last fitness report Major Gray had said I "secure a high degree of loyalty and cooperation from my subordinates." Major Gray had also said, "he secures a high degree of loyalty and cooperation from his subordinates in whom he instills a great sense of personal responsibility for the quality of their work. His subordinates respect him and honor his judgment." For Captain Reinhold to portray any different now was a travesty and a lie. This didn't change in eight months when it was the same people I was working with. The positive Navy Times article was coming back to haunt me.

As I sat there in shock and anger, I asked Captain Reinhold about his comments and if he could give me specifics, who had made negative comments or displayed negative attitudes directed toward me and he couldn't come up with any. I asked him if anyone had come up to him and complained or said that they didn't want to work with me and he replied "well, no." I then asked him if anyone had made any negative comments about me to him or had he ever heard of any from the Marines in the office and his answer was also "no." I couldn't believe it. Here was an officer in the Marine Corps saying something about me with no evidence. Captain Reinhold's characterization of my working relationship with my fellow Marines was in total contradiction to what was reality. I was in shock and disheartened that he could so blatantly lie and I felt all the hard work and long hours that I put in at my unit and the personal relationships that I had built with my Marines was for nothing. It was so blatantly clear that Captain Reinhold wrote this report because of pressure from above affecting his career, and Colonel Fletcher, who was now his boss. There was no reason why, in the same office with the same people my performance evaluation could have gone down. Later on, some of my peers in the office and subordinates heard about the fitness report and were shocked.

The Marine Corps was definitely putting the screws to me and they were fighting back. They didn't like it eight months earlier when it was in the Navy Times and other press that I had been recommended for promotion and they were being seen as being unfair to a good Marine. It was clear because of that prior news article and people high up in the Marines that pressure was on to downgrade my performance. When it came to some people in the Marines, integrity and honor were not part of their character when it came to their prejudices against gays and lesbians.

I was never so happy as the day I walked out of my unit at Marine Corps Base to report over to my new command at Second FSSG to start anew. I did have some trepidation down deep inside but I would just have to push on. It was a new year and a new command.

CHAPTER 18
BURN OUT AND REGRET

1000 hours 28 November 1994 Camp Lejeune, North Carolina

On the morning of November 28, I drove over to the headquarters for the Commanding General Second Force Service Support Group (FSSG) not knowing what unit I would be sent to within the FSSG. After spending about fifteen minutes there I got the paper work to go over to Second Supply Battalion my new unit. As I drove over to Second Supply Battalion, my stomach was in knots as I would have to deal with a whole new command full of Marines and sailors I didn't know, but I was sure that a lot of them would recognize me and have preconceived opinions. Here I was, going into my third year of serving openly in the Marine Corps and after all I had been through, sometimes I just wished that I could be invisible for just one day. Just once I would have liked to walk into a place and for people not to recognize me. It would have been great to be able to relax and not have to go into a room full of Marines and have to deal with a whole spectrum of attitudes, from quietly supportive to openly hostile. It was starting to take toll on my physical health, in the way of stress- related symptoms and it also affected my trying to stay positive when I was always under pressure from those who didn't want me in the Marines. Meeting new Marines could some-times be an edgy situation because of preconceived ideas about me that they might already have before meeting me for the first time. I was professional, comfortable in my own skin and not a push-over or timid, however, some Marines would try to give me attitude or would be difficult to deal with, which ended up sometimes being a battle of wills, but I didn't take flak from anybody.

It bothered some Marines because they saw being gay as shameful, and what I had done by coming out as disloyal and embarrassing to the Marine Corps, but I didn't see it that way at all. Having to deal with these attitudes and feeling like I was in a state of limbo and had hit a glass ceiling was starting to burn me out. I had accepted a couple of things in my mind while at the same time keeping a positive attitude to keep going. Number one, I knew I would never be promoted, as the Marine Corps would not allow it even though I was being recommended for promotion. Number two, I knew that most likely my court case would not be the one to change the military policy on gays, looking at the way some of the other court cases were progressing, specifically Midshipman Joseph Steffan's court case. So I had to ask myself, "why am I still pressing on?" My goal of proving that an openly gay Marine could be successful with no detriment to morale was my goal and why I pressed on.

As I walked into the Second Supply Battalion headquarters that morning I made my way to the Administrative Office to check in. I wasn't the only one at the counter checking in, so I waited my turn. The Marine who helped me was professional. A few minutes later I found out that I would be working at Medical Logistics Company within Second Supply Battalion. I then took my paperwork and drove over to the Medical Logistics Company office and checked in with my boss, Lieutenant Toomey. I would be working as the Fiscal Chief for the company. I fit in right away and most everyone I worked with in the company was cool and easy to work with. Medical Logistics Company was half-and-half, Marines and sailors, and had a Navy Commanding Officer and Executive Officer.

In February, my annual fitness report was due. I had only been with the command three months but I got all "outstandings" across the board in all areas. The Executive Officer wrote:

"Although Sergeant Elzie has only been on board for three months, he has demonstrated superior motivation, dedication to duty and outstanding professional and military performance. Sergeant Elzie is innovative, inquisitive and inventive. His performance as fiscal chief has greatly contributed to the operational readiness of this company ensuring that the command has up to date and accurate accountability of PE and RA funds at all times. His superb working knowledge of fiscal/supply functions, time management, communication skills and overall positive attitude has made the day to day supply operations flow smooth and precise. Sergeant Elzie is the Bachelor Enlisted Quarters NCO and has successfully supervised and coordinated barracks relocations with minimal disruption to the residents. Sergeant Elzie has acted as both Company Gunny and Supply Chief when called upon. He also volunteers his off time with the local County AIDS Task Force. Sergeant Elzie's willingness to perform above and beyond what is normally expected mark him as an excellent candidate for increased responsibility. He is highly recommended for promotion."

After getting this fitness report, some of my stress went away as moving to a new unit gave me a new start with a whole new set of people. I had to constantly prove myself but I saw it as a challenge and it improved my overall health to be in a more welcoming unit that didn't care about who I was, and treated me like every other Marine. I was not always recognized in the battalion though and it sometimes made for interesting situations when people then did realize who I was.

One day I was down at the battalion at the Administrative Office taking care of something for one of my troops and I was standing at the counter as a Staff Sergeant was talking disparagingly about gays right there in front of the whole office and said something about how he had heard that that "gay Sergeant" was now in our Second Supply Battalion and how he would give him a piece of mind if he came across him. As he was saying this he didn't recognize me, or the fact that I was standing right there. The looks on some of the Marines faces were sort of pained as they realized what was happening. The Master Gunnery Sergeant in charge of the office immediately told the Staff Sergeant that he wanted to speak to him outside and took him out of the office. A couple of minutes later the Master Gunnery Sergeant came back in and apologized to me for the Staff Sergeant's homophobic behavior and what he said. I thanked him and was in total shock that this Marine Staff NCO had done the right thing and called the Staff Sergeant out on his behavior. Things had changed for me in the Marine Corps at some levels and one was that I had found new respect over the past year. That day I was so glad to now be with Second Supply Battalion.

In January I talked to my mother on the phone and we had a very lengthy and engaging conversation. We discussed my brother Matthew who was in the Army and who had gotten married recently. I had not been invited to the wedding. I didn't even know that he had gotten married until a few months later. I was quite surprised and deeply hurt that my only brother would not invite me to his wedding. My sister later told me about the wedding and how when she asked why I wasn't there, my brother told her if she brought up my name again he would put her out of the car.

My mother saw nothing wrong with him not inviting me to the wedding. She said that if people like my brother were ostracizing me in the family it was my own fault. In her opinion, their behavior was my own doing, just like how the Marines had said that my coming out impacted my performance because they were trying to kick me out. She mentioned how my cousin Dan and my brother Matthew had both gotten some flak in the military because they were my relatives, but I couldn't see how that excluded them from supporting me. My family as a whole blamed me for other people's attitudes and homophobic behaviors—just as the Marines were.

To my family it was my fault because I didn't keep my mouth shut.

This didn't sit well with me at all. The way I saw it was you stand by your family. Especially since I hadn't done anything wrong, turning their backs on me was cowardly and dishonorable. It just reinforced to me who my real family was—my gay friends who didn't turn their backs on me. My mother with her pious Christian attitude, in the course of the conversation said I was "abnormal" because I was gay. Needless to say, I was incensed and upset by the end of the call. I don't know why I kept hoping that my parents and family would come around to accepting me. I just needed to accept that I would never, no matter how many years went by, have the relationship that I hoped with my parents or my brother. My sister was the only one in the family who was supportive.

In early 1995, I was part of a project done by Apollo Media, run by Clinton Fein who had put together a CD in partnership with the famous author Randy Shilts, based on his book, *Conduct Unbecoming, Gays and Lesbians in the U.S. Military*. This CD had a few interviews and stories of gay servicemembers on it. It was release and sold through *Wired Magazine*. It had a bit of my story on it with pictures. I hoped by being a part of it that it would tell our story and help educate people.

In March of 1996, my good friend Perry Watkins died. He was an amazing person and as a gay, African American soldier, he was one of the first servicemembers to have success in defying the ban on gays in the military. I knew as I went through my days after this that Perry was in heaven looking down giving us all encouragement. I loved his "pulling not punches" attitude. He was a good friend and mentor.

In early June, John and I were thinking of going to Pride in North Carolina if we had the money, but we both had to work. We also were thinking of going to Pride in Washington, D.C. and to the oral arguments in my court case scheduled for June 29, but that all changed when I found out that I had the opportunity to go on an exercise aboard ship.

There was a three-week Capability Exercise, (CAPEX) and they needed some volunteers. I put in for it and I was approved. I would be going as the Platoon Sergeant. I called one of my attorneys, Chris, to let him know that I would be going on a ship for this exercise but I would still be able to be at the oral arguments for my case, Elzie v. Perry in front of Federal District Judge Stanley Sporkin on July 11, 1995. He thought it was great and it would just make the government's argument look stupid as here they were trying to kick me out but they were at the same time sending me on an exercise on a ship where they said in the close quarters gays and lesbians could cause detriment to morale. I just looked at it as just another challenge and opportunity to prove that gays and lesbians were compatible in the military. I kept thinking of the to- do Senators Sam Nunn and Dan Coats had made of the bunks on the ship during the Senate hearings on gays in the military.

As soon as I got approved to go I called John immediately. When I told John he sounded surprised. Over the next few days I told a few friends, most seemed happy that I was going. There was one friend of mine who was gay and a Navy Corpsman who did not think it was a good idea. Some people go out on ships and never come back, especially if they are not liked, they disappear, overboard. Then the excuse was "well he must have accidently fell overboard." The whole talk about this didn't scare me as I had realized early on that I couldn't be worried about my personal safety and that I just needed to march on and keep my goals in focus. I think though as the time grew nearer for me to go, John got worried and didn't want me to go.

On June 19, 1995, we left in several vans from Second FSSG in Lejeune to drive to Norfolk, Virginia to board the USS NASSAU. Once we got to Norfolk we boarded the ship and settled in. I was the Detachment Non Commissioned Officer in Charge, (NCIOC) for the FSSG team, which included Marines and sailors from Second Supply Battalion and Second Medical Battalion, so I had to set up schedules, duty rosters, track equipment for static displays and attend meetings. I had to deal with the Marines from the other units on the ship that were from Second Marine Division, which included Tankers and Grunts.

I pretty much got along with everyone, except one of the Platoon Sergeants from Division. It was obvious that he had a problem with me being gay by the attitude that he tried to give me. We butted heads sometimes but in the end it all worked out as we just kept to our separate units. Our Mission for the CAPEX was that we were going to do schedule port visits to Halifax, Nova Scotia (23-28 June) and Boston Massachusetts for Harborfest 95 (1-5 July). Our unit was to set up static displays on board to provide the public an opportunity to observe the unique abilities of the USS NASSAU in supporting the Navy-Marine Corps Team. Once we got on ship and settled in I got to work and was responsible for holding formations and passing information as the leader of our unit.

Getting ready for this CAPEX I knew that I would need to bring something to read to pass the time when we had down time on the ship. I brought along a book that I was reading at the time: "Makes Me Wanna Holler: A Young Black Man in America" by Nathan McCall. The reason I was reading this book was, as I mentioned, since coming out I had noticed that most of the positive support I got from Marines was usually more from African American and Hispanic Marines than white Marines. I found myself identifying more and more with the discrimination that African Americans go through. The same feelings, attitudes and consequences are outcomes when one has to deal with discrimination. Discrimination is discrimination whether it is based on race, gender or sexual orientation.

After reading the book and going through what I had to go through I really thought that if more straight white male Ma-

213

rines had to deal with the discrimination (racism, sexism, and homophobia) that minorities go through it would change a lot of peoples' thinking.

It was a very successful exercise aboard the USS NASSUA and on July 7, my 33rd birthday we pulled back into port in Norfolk, Virginia and got in vans back to Camp Lejeune.

Right after I got back from this exercise on the ship I got my annual fitness report. It again was all "outstandings" across the board in leadership, judgment, loyalty and handling personnel. Lieutenant Toomey wrote on my evaluation:

"Sergeant Elzie continues to set the standard by which excellence is measured. He has proven himself to be very reliable and accurate. His superb working knowledge of both the Medlog Supply and fiscal Systems has increased the operational of the Medical Logistics Company. He performs his duties as Fiscal Chief, is a dedicated cheerful and hard-working manner. He has the ability to adapt to change when called upon, demonstrating both versatility and managerial skills. His positive attitude during times of crises has generated enthusiasm at all levels within this company. He reorganized the fiscal shop, resulting in an up-todate financial picture, so his superiors can procure needed items immediately. He has continually demonstrated he has the ability to develop and organize procedures that weigh resources while ensuring the most effective and economic method is applied. Sergeant Elzie is the Bachelor Enlisted Quarters NCO and devotes numerous extra hours to ensure all problems were taken care of followed-up on any unresolved actions. His total commitment to the Marine Corps, support of his superiors and leadership of subordinates have enhanced readiness, retention and morale. He is most strongly recommended for promotion to Staff Sergeant. I would be pleased to have him work with me at any duty station."

On July 11, I took the day off and made the trip up to Washington, D.C. for the Oral Arguments in my court case Elzie v. Perry.

It was a sunny day and very formal as I sat in the courtroom and heard the arguments in front of Judge Sporkin. Christopher Sipes argued that the government's policy of excluding homosexuals is unconstitutional. He argued that they should restore my eligibility for active duty in the Marine Corps with all of the rights, and benefits, like every other Marine and they should restore my full participation in the Voluntary Separation Incentive and Special Separation Benefit (VSI/SSB) program. The oral arguments didn't last long and as soon as we walked out of the courthouse the press asked several questions.

Christopher said to the press that Judge Stanley Sporkin is a federal judge who has a reputation as one of the brightest sitting justices. He went on to say: "It's impossible to predict how long Sporkin will deliberate, but my preference is that he take as long as he needs to consider fully all the aspects of this case. This is a complicated case, and the first to interpret Steffan. While you can never, and I mean never predict what a judge will decide, I believe Judge Sporkin is open minded on this issue and is willing to consider the case on its own merits." When they asked me what I thought I said I was optimistic about the legal battle and I was pleased that I had been supported by my immediate supervisors. Coming out of the courtroom after hearing the arguments was not as bad as the day that I sat through my discharge hearing, but it had some of the same elements where my future and character were up for discussion. It is not an easy thing to sit in a courtroom and listen as one side tries to demonize you about something that you don't see as wrong or that shouldn't be an issue.

During these oral arguments I was once again reminded how much I owed Chris, Lanny and Allan for all the work and support they did for me on this case. At times they were my only support and lifeline keeping my optimism up.

On August 14, Judge Sporkin issued his opinion in our favor and the government appealed it. Judge Sporkin, in his Memorandum Opinion made several good points. One point in particular was, "This case now comes before the Court on cross-motions for summary judgment. Despite his exemplary record, the military remains committed to denying Sergeant Elzie benefits under the VSI/SSB program and continues to seek Sergeant Elzie's discharge. The irony of the current posture of this litigation is not lost on this Court. Plaintiff was ready and willing to leave the military voluntarily by April 1993 as long as he was permitted to participate in the VSI/SSB program. He had already been accepted into the program and had met the eligibility criteria. The military has prolonged Sergeant Elzie's stay in the Marine Corps due to its need to enforce its discharge policy. It would appear that the military is not simply seeking to discharge Sergeant Elzie due to the purported threat to military morale and discipline, but is also seeking to punish Sergeant Elzie by denying him all benefits that a heterosexual, who has served his country in a far less distinguished fashion, is entitled to receive."

Judge Sporkin went on to say that, "This matter comes before the Court on cross-motions for summary judgment. The Court hereby orders that the case be remanded with instructions that Plaintiff's status in the Marine Corps and eligibility for the VSI/SSB program be reviewed under the military's current policy as codified at 10 U.S.C. Section 654."

I was ecstatic in hearing the ruling in the case because he basically laid it out that I had been approved before for the VSI/SSB retirement program and there was no reason that the Marine Corps should try to take that away from me, just because I had said I was gay. The government still appealed.

In October, 1995, John's enlistment contract was up and he decided not to reenlist in the Marines. As soon as he got out we decided to move back off base so that we could be together. I moved out of the barracks and we got a trailer out in town. It was nice again being able to be with him again off base. In November, 1995,

216

the end of my enlistment contract was up but with the ongoing court case, the Marine Corps would not let me reenlist normally. They had made sure I didn't get promoted so that they could say I wasn't qualified for reenlistment. In the message from Headquarters Marine Corps dated November 14, they said that I was unqualified for service in the Marine Corps. So Headquarters Marine Corps directed them to extend my enlistment with an unspecified date until the completion of the court case. Just another example of the limbo that I was in. Other than this, things were going well at work and the end of 1995, Christmas and New Year's came on a good note.

1996 was a blur of a year that was just day-to-day work. Sometimes it felt as though I had been forgotten as I settled into my work and taking care of my troops. In April, I went on a field exercise with my unit and once again was in charge of Marines out in the field and was in foxholes and tents and showers with other Marines and sailors with no problems. In April some of the news media did an update story of my case. Of course, the story was that I continued to serve with no problems, yet the Marine Corps was still refusing to give me the retirement program and trying to kick me out. My attorney Chris was quoted in the press as saying: "Everyday he serves is a victory. It just demonstrates that the whole policy doesn't make sense."

In May I got another Fitness Report. I again was rated with "outstandings" across the board in all areas, including leadership, loyalty, judgment, and handling troops. Lieutenant Mack wrote on my fitness report:

"Sergeant Elzie is one of the most dedicated Marines I have ever served with. A superior leader, manager, and organizer, his potential to the Marine Corps is unlimited. Working as the Supply Chief, he continues to apply strategic management concepts on a variety of duties. His experience and expertise are demonstrated in the flawless maintenance of the DASF, PE/RA Funds, warehousing and accountability of over 1,200 line items. Sergeant Elzie also co-ordinates the Self Service, Open Purchase, and Self Help accounts for the company. As Company Platoon Sergeant, he exhibits exceptional problem solving ability and an outstanding attitude enabling him to satisfy the needs of his troops while accomplishing the mission. Sergeant Elzie has proven his readiness for increased responsibility and is highly recommended for promotion to Staff Sergeant."

I was really happy being at Medical Logistics Company because I had supportive superiors and I really liked my job with my troops and I tried to give 110%. I was starting to hope that the courts would rule that the Marine Corps would have to reenlist me and promote me; however I knew that was a long shot.

In October of 1996, I attended the SLDN's Fourth Annual "End the Witch Hunts" dinner in Washington, D.C., as I was on the Honorary Committee. SLDN was still taking hundreds of calls from servicemembers whom the military was still trying to follow, investigate and discharge.

One case in particular which I knew about was my friend Bryan Clark, who was a Staff Sergeant. We had known each other at Camp Lejeune. In 1996 he was stationed in Hawaii and got out on his regular enlistment and went back home to Texas. In the meantime, there was a gay Air Force servicemember also stationed in Hawaii who was threatened by the Air Force Criminal Investigative Division, (CID) to turn in names of other gay people he knew. Bryan was one of them. Later the CID turned Bryan's name over to Naval Criminal Investigative Service, (NCIS) and they proceeded to call him back on active duty and flew him from Texas back to Hawaii just to investigate him and to find other gays in the military. This was a well documented "Witchhunt" that happened in Hawaii at the time that violated "Don't Ask, Don't Tell." SLDN was tracking it and trying to help servicemembers caught up in this investigation. Bryan was irreparably harmed by the investigation. While he did get an Honorable discharge, he also got a reenlistment code of "RE4," which meant he couldn't go back into the Marines if he wanted to. This again just reminded me of why I was serving and fighting this policy, so that I could somehow change it. It pissed me off that the military was still treating gay and lesbian service members like this.

On November 8, I went to the annual Marine Corps Ball. It was nice but at the same time I felt a little detached. Somehow, I was starting to see that not only had I moved beyond where my fellow gay and lesbian Marines were, I felt also ahead of straight Marines I knew in the Corps. By coming out I had changed myself and how I was looked at by other Marines, and I was forever changed. It was a nice Marine Corps Ball but in the end I was glad to leave and I could see that at some point I needed to move on, soon, with my life. I had outgrown the Marine Corps.

In December, my attorney, Christopher Sipes, called me and we had a long talk. The government had reached out to start negotiating a settlement in our case. Right before Christmas, Chris forwarded me a draft copy of the settlement. The Marine Corps was willing to go ahead and give me my benefits under the VSI/SSB program. However, I would have to sign and agree that upon signing the settlement agreement I would never attempt to reenlist or to seek to serve in the Armed Forces of the United States again. That kind of took me back. Yes I was ready to move on but taking away that option was a jolt. What if I finished college and then wanted to go back in? It was a double-edged sword. I felt conflicted, but in the end I agreed and told Chris to proceed with the negotiation. The papers were signed by the attorneys right after Christmas. That New Year's was bitter-sweet as I knew my time in the Marine Corps, after fourteen years, was coming to a close. I did a lot of soul searching.

In February the news came down that the agreement had been approved by all parties and that I would be discharged effective

February 18, 1997. When the message came down I checked in at the administrative office at 2nd Supply Battalion and started checking out. I had a week before I would be discharged.

In the mean time I got my final fitness report. I got "outstanding" marks across the board in all areas, including leadership, loyalty, judgment and handling troops. Lieutenant Mack wrote on my fitness report:

"During this period Sergeant Elzie performed his duty as Fiscal Chief in an outstanding and exemplary manner. His performance has greatly contributed to the operational readiness of this company. He was instrumental in acquiring and initiating a computer accounting program to improve Medical Logistics Company's accounting procedures, thereby eliminating wasteful spending. He also audited, analyzed and managed a

2 million budget for the past 3 fiscal years. His communication skills and overall positive attitude has set a high standard for Marines and sailors alike. While acting as Platoon Sergeant he demonstrated the leadership abilities that are needed to lead the Marine Corps into the 21st century. His dedication to duty is unquestioned. He has devoted numerous arduous hours to ensure mission accomplishment."

After reading this I thought it was ironic because I wouldn't be around here for the 21st century in the Marine Corps.

Tuesday, February 18, came quickly and it was a day when yes, I was happy to be moving on because I was burnt-out but at the same time I was sad and feeling regret. I was now ending a career that I had for fourteen years. I felt that I had made a difference, but I hadn't changed the Marine Corps like I had wanted to do. I proved that a Marine who happens to be gay can serve just as well as a Marine who happens to be straight, with no detriment to morale, or impact to mission operation. But to me, at the end of the day, it wasn't enough. I hadn't finished my mission. It was like a hollow or incomplete victory in some respects, because the ban on gays in the military was still there. However, I felt at the end of the day, strong mentally and physically and that I had made it through the fire.

The biggest personal victory out of all of this was that I had earned the title of a United States Marine. I had played by their rules, I happened to be gay; I proved that you could serve openly, and I succeeded at that. I walked away with my dignity and self-worth and as the saying goes, "Once a Marine, always a Marine." At the end of the day, nobody could take that away from me.

EPILOGUE

This book has been about my life up to the point I left the Marine Corps. After serving in the Marines for fourteen years, which included four years as an out gay man, thirteen years ago I had to take a break. John and I eventually broke up and went our separate ways but still remain close friends to this day. The stress of "Don't Ask, Don't Tell" and how we both changed affected our relationship beyond repair.

Ironically, my relationship with my parents today can be described as "Don't Ask, Don't Tell." While we are on good terms, and I love them, I still hope to have their complete acceptance someday without bigoted Christian judgment. Still, I find myself everyday becoming my father in many ways, and of that I am proud. I respect my father and hope that someday he will—with no judgment—be proud of what I have become in this life.

Over the past year I have lobbied Congress and helped organize rallies, all in support of the repeal of "Don't Ask, Don't Tell." I have also written extensively about "Don't Ask, Don't Tell" and how the strategy and the lack of action by President Obama in stopping the discharges is shameful. I have written about how President Obama, the Commander in Chief of the Armed Forces, is letting the military control this issue, even though he has the power to issue a "stop loss" order to end the discharges.

I feel like I am seeing 1993 happen all over again, with yet another politician firing outstanding servicemembers and throwing the LGBT community under the bus. Arabic linguists like Lieutenant Dan Choi, highly-decorated jet fighter pilots like Lieutenant Colonel Victor Fehrenbach, and many other servicemembers in critical jobs that are needed to fight America's enemies are being fired by President Obama.

Harvey Milk once said: "It takes no compromising to give people their rights. It takes no money to respect the individual. It takes no survey to remove repressions."

President Obama's excuse of wanting to execute repeal in an "orderly way" is political doublespeak and appeasement toward those in the military hierarchy who want to delay indefinitely the repeal of this discriminatory policy. He could sign an order tomorrow stopping discharges and the military would continue to function professionally with no problems. As an example, the overnight lifting of the ban on gays in the British military resulted in no disruption of their military. My own story, of serving as an out gay man in the United States Marine Corps, with no impact on unit cohesion or morale, is another. Today the United States is now in the same select group of countries (North Korea, Iran, Cuba, Saudi Arabia, etc.), which have human rights violations and support terrorism, and at the same time discriminate against LGBT Servicemembers. All the original NATO countries, with the exception of the United States and Turkey, now allow LGBT Servicemembers to serve in the armed forces without discrimination.

This past year I wrote about how, if the President had issued a "stop loss" order ending the discharges (which he has the power to do under Title 10, United States Code, Section 12305) when he came into office, this would have taken away the main claim about problems with showers and foxholes, that opponents of repeal use to continue to support "Don't Ask, Don't Tell." By allowing LGBT Servicemembers to serve without being discharged until Congress repealed "Don't Ask, Don't Tell" would have built the case that the military would not fall apart during a time of war with openly gay servicemembers, and it would have taken away a point in the debate out of the hands of the proponents of "Don't Ask, Don't Tell." When it came time for "Don't Ask, Don't Tell" to come up in Congress for repeal the president then could have easily pointed to the fact that the military had continued to perform professionally and successfully in time of war with openly gay servicemembers. He could have, for instance, pointed out that no gay Arabic linguists had been kicked out, thereby not hurting national security. But now because he has not issued a 'stop-loss" for political reasons and based it on the need of national security to not kick out Arabic linguists (like he said during his campaign,) he has in effect undermined his own argument on the national security point, by not taking action. Today President Obama has already fired over 400 servicemembers.

Also sadly, the President has appealed Judge Virgina Phillips decision, that "Don't Ask, Don't Tell" is unconstitutional, in the federal lawsuit, Log Cabin Republicans vs. United States of America. Obama is aggressively fighting against the repeal of "Don't Ask, Don't Tell" through the courts. A majority of Constitutional Scholars and even the National Law Journal have all pointed out that his administration did not have to appeal the judge's decision. The Obama administration's talking point that the Department of Justice must defend all laws is simply not true. When Judge Phillips decision was issued the Department of Defense complied and for eight days there was no "Don't Ask, Don't Tell" with no "Enormous Consequences" as Secretary of Defense, Robert Gates had said there would be. President Obama has gone above and beyond to reinstate "Don't Ask, Don't Tell" after it was declared unconstitutional and dead for eight days. President Obama now has the unique distinction of being the only President to reinstate an unconstitutional law against LGBT Servicemembers after the military with a groundbreaking development officially started accepting them at recruiting stations.

President Obama has said he is a "fierce advocate for gay and lesbian Americans," but if you ask any United States Marine, or any drag queen, the definition of "fierce" you're going to get a couple of pretty good definitions, none of which exemplifies this administration.

It is also extremely sad to see the current Commandant of the Marine Corps, General Amos state that he is for keeping this discriminatory policy. He said, "There is a risk involved," in repealing Don't Ask Don't Tell. His statement ignores all evidence to the contrary. We need a Commandant of the Marine Corps who is a leader that values all of his troops, and will uphold the highest standards of ethics, and conduct when it comes to non-discrimination.

My love for the Marine Corps, for wanting to see it move into the twenty-first century in respect to how it treats its LGBT servicemembers is unwavering. I will continue to speak out when the Marine Corps doesn't live up to its ideals of promoting a diverse, quality force that it says is essential to progress and mission accomplishment. It is hypocritical for an organization to claim to fight for the freedoms of all Americans while at the same time discriminating against a whole group of Americans already in its ranks.

President Obama's lack of support for our equality will not dampen the spirit of the many LGBT Servicemembers, veterans or activists working on this issue. This movement is bigger than one man, organization or institution. We will win in the end on this issue; that I guarantee you.

My hope in writing this book is that it becomes part of the conversation getting rid of the ban on gays in the military and makes a positive difference in people's lives. Right now I feel more determined than ever to finish the mission that I started seventeen years ago, to change the Marine Corps for the better, and to stop the discrimination against my LGBT sisters and brothers in the military. I hope this book does that.

Justin Crockett Elzie
November 2010

Earlier this year while I was riding on the New York City subway, I wrote a poem expressing my feelings about President Obama, the politician, and how many people are naively taken in by his lofty words but lack of action on this issue.

Naivety

Warm blood
Stomach tight
Shaking with emotion
Feels like my head will explode.

Wide smile
Eloquent speech
Repeated words
People cheer.

Sits on hands
Cocktail parties
Repeated words
People cheer.

Pass the buck
Military's in charge
Repeated words
People cheer.

Backroom deals
Points the finger
Repeated words
People cheer.

Warm blood

Stomach tight
Shaking with emotion
Sheep led to the slaughter.